Flow as a Resource:

A Contribution to Organizational Psychology

Lisa Vivoll Straume

Master thesis in Psychology

Department of Psychology, NTNU Spring 2004

Flow as a Resource:

A Contribution to Organizational Psychology

Lisa Vivoll Straume

Department of Psychology,
Norwegian University of Science and Technology
Trondheim, Norway
Spring 2004

© Tapir Akademisk Forlag, Trondheim 2008

ISBN 978-82-519-2310-1

Det må ikke kopieres fra denne boka ut over det som er tillatt etter bestemmelser i lov om opphavsrett til åndsverk, og avtaler om kopiering inngått med Kopinor.

Digitaltrykk og innbinding: Tapir Uttrykk

Tapir Akademisk Forlag
7005 TRONDHEIM

Tlf.: 73 59 32 10
Faks: 73 59 84 94
E-post: forlag@tapir.no
www.tapirforlag.no

PREFACE

Dear Reader,

You hold in your hands the result of a process that first commenced when I attended a psychology class back in springtime 2000. During this class, Professor Maria Lewica introduced to me the notion of flow experiences in one of her lectures. I can clearly remember being totally absorbed and carried away by her talking, it was something about this phenomenon that captured my attention entirely. I could easily relate the feeling of flow to my personal repertoire, and as time went by, I started searching for ways to increase my own flow experiences. A strong desire grew in me to learn more about the flow state, and to understand how we could utilize the inherent resources incorporated in the flow state. The master thesis of my graduate degree in psychology was my first opportunity to put my ideas into action. This master thesis simply stems from my desire to empirically investigate what flow is and how it relates to the working individual.

The entire thesis consists of an introductory article and two empirical research articles that are built on the theoretical basis made introductory. The theoretical foundation of the project is more comprehensive than what has been empirically tested in the research articles. Yet, I considered it necessary to establish a thorough framework of the flow theory prior to empirically testing it. Due to the structure of the thesis, some reiteration will occur, and I apologize for the inconvenience this may cause. In most cases, the text is formatted in APA style, apart from minor exceptions. Due to the size of the thesis, numbers have been applied to headings in order to make it easier for the reader to stay oriented. To keep the format consistent, it was decided to continue the numbered headings in all three articles.

I owe my thanks to several people for making this thesis a final product. First of all, to all the respondents, you made this possible. Thanks also to Jan Fjeldsæter at Total Consult, who kindly agreed to cooperate on the data collection process. To all my co-students, I have sought my inspiration through you. I also want to thank Inger and Bjørg-Elin for helpful comments on a draft version, and to Frode and Kjetil for always curing my computer when it crashed. To Ida Kortner Hasting, for making me a better person. May you rest in peace.

Special thanks go to my supervisor Torbjørn Rundmo for always being there when I needed guidance and supervising. You have been an important inspiration in my desire to become a skilled scientist. Thanks also to Joar Vittersø, for helping me to conduct the flow simplex analysis and for your useful advices. Your knowledge is so valuable to me, and I really look forward to cooperate with you on my doctoral dissertation the next four years ahead. Last but not least, I want to thank my parents for the love and care you have given me through all my years of studying, and for always believing in me and my work. To Kristin, my dearest sister, you are my soul-mate, my best friend, my inspiration. Finally, special thanks goes to Erlend for bearing with me and supporting me through my ups and downs. I love you to the deepest of my heart.

Trondheim, 28.05.2004
Lisa Vivoll Straume

CONTENTS

PREFACE	V
CONTENTS	VII
ABSTRACT	XI

INTRODUCTION ARTICLE

1.0 Psychological Flow as a Resource: A Contribution to Organizational Psychology	15
1.1 The project: Flow as a natural resource	15
1.2 Contents	15
1.3 Theoretical foundation of the project	16
1.3.1 Psychological flow – the optimal experience	17
1.3.2 Conceptualizing flow through scheme theory	20
1.3.3 Empirically testing affective responses to assimilation resistance	22
1.3.4 Integrating flow in goal setting theory	23
1.4 Towards a unified theory of flow in organizational psychology	30
1.4.1 Prerequisites of flow	31
1.4.2 Immediate experiential characteristics of flow	32
1.4.3 Subsequent consequences of flow	33
1.5 Theoretical foundation for work motivation, work performance, and job satisfaction	33
1.5.1 Psychological flow and work motivation	33
1.5.2 Psychological flow and job satisfaction	35
1.5.3 Psychological flow and work performance	35
1.6 Aims of the thesis	36
1.6.1 Specific aims of 1st article	36
1.6.2 Specific aims of 2nd article	37
2.0 Method	38
2.1 Sample	38

2.2 Procedure	38
2.3 Questionnaire	38
2.3.1 General part of the questionnaire	39
2.3.2 Specific part of the questionnaire	40
2.4 Statistical analyses	40
3.0 Results	41
3.1 Main results of 1st article	41
3.2 Main results of 2nd article	42
4.0 Discussion and implications	42
4.1 Measuring the flow experience	42
4.2 Flow experiences at work	44
4.3 The role of goal setting in flow experiences	45
4.4 Using flow as a resource to increase work motivation, work performance, and job satisfaction	46
4.4.1 Psychological flow and work motivation	47
4.4.2 Psychological flow and work performance	47
4.4.3 Psychological flow and job satisfaction	48
4.5 Practical implications	48
4.6 Conclusion: Applicability of results	49
References	52

1st ARTICLE

ABSTRACT	59
1.0 Flow, work motivation, and goal setting	61
1.1 The flow construct	61
1.2 The flow state scale revised	63
1.3 Psychological flow and work motivation	63
1.4 Goal setting as a predictor of flow experiences	64
1.5 Aims of the study	66

2.0 Method	67
2.1 Sample	67
2.2 Questionnaire	67
2.3 Statistical analyses	68
3.0 Results	69
3.1 Dimensional structure and reliability of the Flow State Scale	69
3.2 Dimensional structure and reliability of motivation and satisfaction	74
3.3 Factors related to work motivation	74
3.4 Psychological flow and goal setting	76
4.0 Discussion	77
References	83

2nd ARTICLE

ABSTRACT	89
1.0 Flow in work situations	91
1.1 Theoretical approaches to the flow construct	91
1.2 Conceptualizing flow through scheme theory	92
1.3 Empirically testing the flow state of assimilation resistance	93
1.4 Psychological flow and work motivation	95
1.5 Psychological flow and job satisfaction	96
1.6 Psychological flow and work performance	97
1.7 Aims of the paper	97
2.0 Method	99
2.1 Sample	99
2.2 Questionnaire	99
2.3 Statistical analyses	101
3.0 Results	101

3.1 The flow experience	101
3.2 The flow simplex in four work situations	101
3.2.1 Flow simplex in four situations	102
3.2.2 The experience of being in flow at work	103
3.2.3 The experience of not having enough time to finish a work task	104
3.2.4 The experience of having plenty of time to finish a work task	105
3.2.5 The experience of not reaching a set goal at work	106
3.3 Experiential effects of four situations	107
4.0 Discussion	108
References	113

APPENDIXES

APPENDIX A: Correlation matrix of the flow simplex variables – 2nd article	117
APPENDIX B: Questionnaire	121

Abstract

The purpose of the present master thesis was to investigate if and how the state of psychological flow can be used as a resource in organizational psychology. A theoretical foundation of flow was established before testing the model empirically. The respondents were workers recruited from nine companies located in the Municipality of Trondheim in middle Norway. The 170 participants represented occupations from a variety of fields, including technology, financial departments, medical business, social services, and salesmen. Based on the theoretical evaluation and empirical analyses, results indicate that goal setting can be a predictor of flow experiences at work. At work, flow is experienced as fun and interesting, which differ slightly from other studies who have found flow to be characterized as challenging. The effects of being in flow can be attributed to increased work motivation, work performance, and job satisfaction. Implications regarding measurements of flow are discussed, and suggestions regarding the future research and applicability of the flow model are made.

Introduction Article

Master Thesis in Psychology
Lisa Vivoll Straume

Department of Psychology, Norwegian University of Science and Technology
Trondheim, Norway
Spring 2004

1.0 Psychological Flow as a Resource: A Contribution to Organizational Psychology

1.1 The project: Flow as a natural resource

A common characteristic of what we view as good, interesting and emotional satisfactory occurrences is the state of mind called psychological flow. Flow is a state of profound task-absorption and intrinsic enjoyment. The flow experience breeds a feeling of coping, makes us more efficient, and is generally considered to be a highly motivating and satisfactory state of mind (Csikszentmihalyi & Csikszentmihalyi 1992; Csikszentmihalyi 2003; Kowal & Fortier, 1999). Although most people are unaware of its presence, flow is a natural part of our every day life. Previous research has proven the flow experience to be clearly related to processes of motivation, performance, and satisfaction in a number of areas, including sports, leisure, and educational research (Jackson & Marsh, 1996; Jackson, Thomas, Marsh, & Smethurst, 2001; Kowal & Fortier, 1999; Marr, 2001). Although this relation has not been tested directly in work settings, it follows that flow may function as a potential resource employees may use to increase work motivation, job satisfaction and work performance. Based on this assumption, two primary aims constitute the present thesis. The first main aim is to build a practically useful theory of goal setting and flow that is functional in organizational psychological research. The second primary aim of this thesis is to empirically test the flow theory in relation to goal setting, work motivation, work performance, and job satisfaction. Hopefully, the thesis will also stimulate to further research through making readers aware of the natural resource that lies in the flow experience.

1.2 Contents

The thesis consists of the present introductory paper and two independent empirical research articles. This introductory article provides a detailed presentation of the theoretical framework in which a theory of flow can complement organizational psychology. The first article aims at validating the Flow State Scale (FSS) to fit data collection in work settings. Consequently, flow will be analyzed in relation to work motivation and goal setting in a comparison analysis of two different versions of the FSS. The second article examines the flow experience in four specific work situations, i.e. absorbed in the task at hand, time pressure, time sufficiency, and not succeeding in reaching a set goal. These four situations are analyzed in relation to work performance, work motivation, and job satisfaction. The flow variable of the second paper is tested using a flow simplex structure, which is based on a different statistical arithmetic than regular questionnaires. The flow simplex structure has earlier proven to be particularly sensitive to variations in the flow experience. The logic behind this method will be elaborated later in the text.

1.3 Theoretical foundation of the project

For the purpose of clarity, the flow concept is here defined as a mental state. Flow can also be understood through a social constructivist view, as an experience existing only through the interaction of personal and situational factors. However, the main interest of this thesis is to gain an understanding of the individual experience of flow, and how it influences factors such as work motivation and work performance. Furthermore, it is of interest to investigate the effects personal goal setting have on the personal experience of flow. Thus, this thesis will solely discuss flow as a mental state, understood as the subjective encounter of an optimal experience.

The flow concept was first introduced by Csikszentmihalyi (1975a) after several research projects trying to understand what made people happy. Interestingly, studies around the world have shown that regardless of age, gender, ethnical background, or education, people report the same state in whatever context they feel a deep sense of enjoyment. What people do in the moment of enjoyment is wildly different, they may be singing opera, writing research articles, performing surgery, or closing a deal – but what they *feel* at the moment is remarkably consistent. The word flow was given to this experience because so many had used the analogy of being carried away, of "moving effortlessly with a current of energy", at the moments of highest enjoyment (Csikszentmihalyi, 2003 p. 39).

Although the research of Csikszentmihalyi and his associates have brought us to an important understanding of how the flow state function, it still lacks the depth a psychometric psychological concept calls for (Marr, 2001). First of all, the characteristics of flow ought to be organized in a way that distinguishes between prerequisites, experiential consequences, and subsequent effects of flow. By now, flow is usually described without distinguishing between prior and subsequent characteristics (Csikszentmihalyi & Csikszentmihalyi, 1992; Jackson & Marsh, 1996; Massimini & Carli, 1992). Second, a more sophisticated theoretical clarification of how the subconscious mind works during the flow state is needed. In order to compensate for this lack, Eckblad's (1981) scheme theory will be used complementarily.

Furthermore, to build a more accurate and applicable theory of flow that fits organizational psychology, Locke and Latham's (1990, 1997, 2002) theory on goal setting is viewed as an important contribution. Goal setting theory may serve to explain important prerequisites for entering the flow state. Before introducing these additional contributions, the definition of flow as given by Csikszentmihalyi and his associates will be presented.

1.3.1 Psychological flow – the optimal experience.

Flow can be defined as a state of mind where you become one with what you are doing, that is, a merging of the self and the action at hand. It is a state of mind where the fixed distinction between the self and the surroundings fade away, where we act intuitively without any clear divergence between stimulus and responses. The sense of time becomes distorted, blurring the more common distinction between past, present and future. Furthermore, the flow state does not require conscious participation by the person who is acting. Yet, the person acts at the fullest level of performance. The attention is focused on a limited area of stimuli, centered on one thing, here and now (Csikszentmihalyi & Csikszentmihalyi, 1992; Kowal & Fortier, 1999; Mitchell, 1992).

Csikszentmihalyi and Csikszentmihalyi (1992) and Jackson and Marsh (1996) have identified nine characteristics that describe and constitute the factors necessary to enter and sustain the flow state. These are presented below.

Challenge – Skill balance. An important prerequisite for the flow state is the match between skills and challenges. When the challenges of a task grow too high, one gets frustrated, worried or eventually anxious. On the other hand, if both challenges and skills are low, we are left feeling bored or even apathetic. However, when both challenges and skills are high, i.e. in line with what is perceived as being just about manageable, then flow is likely to occur (Csikszentmihalyi, 1997). In one of his first books on psychological flow, Csikszentmihalyi (1975a) describes flow as a state of mind between boredom and anxiety. The person acting needs to continuously sustain the equilibrium of skill and challenge in order to avoid boredom or anxiety. In flow, we sort of linger in between those very loosely set phases, which often produce a highly pleasurable feeling. A schematic illustration of the challenge-skill balance is given below in Figure 1.

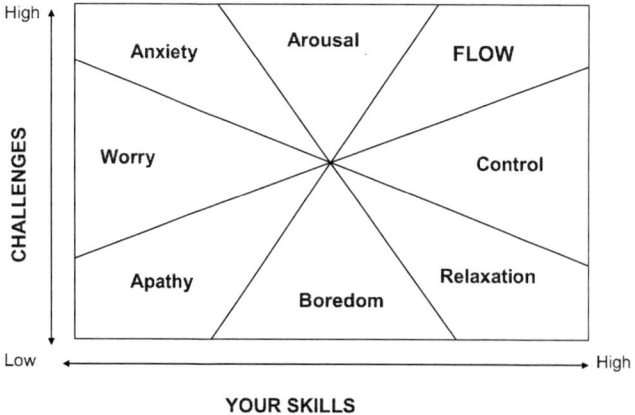
Figure 1. Challenge-skill balance

Action–Awareness Merging. The flow state implies a total involvement of the activity, often referred to as becoming one with what you are doing. Because we invest all our psychic energy in accomplishing the task at hand, flow implies a total involvement with the activity. This involvement results in a merging of the self and the action at hand. As argued by Jackson and Marsh (1996), "there is no awareness of self as separate from the actions one is performing" (p. 18).

Clear goals. The goals of the activity need to be clearly defined in order to sustain the flow state. If the goals are set in advance, they function as rules for action that make it possible for the person to perform without questioning what should be done. Goals can also develop out of the involvement in the activity, thus providing information about appropriate responses. Consider the pianist as an example. In playing Rachmaninov's 3rd, he or she simply knows by heart what the next notes are, and does not have to consciously appraise what the next chord to play is. Csikszentmihalyi specifies that it is the immediate goals ever present in the activity that are crucial for the flow experience (Csikszentmihalyi 2003, p. 42).

Unambiguous feedback. While in flow, immediate and clear feedback is continuously received by the person. As pointed out by Csikszentmihalyi (1993), "it is difficult for people to stay absorbed in any activity unless they get timely, "online" information about how well they are doing" (Csikszentmihalyi 2003, p. 43). This allows the person to know that he or she is succeeding in reaching the set goal. If the pianist hits the wrong chord, flow is interrupted.

Sense of control. The feedback discussed above brings about a feeling of coping, a feeling of being in control of your actions. Interestingly, the person does not actively try to exert control; it merges as a consequence of the internal feedback described above.

Concentration on task at hand. All distractions are excluded from the consciousness as long as the person sustains the flow experience. Flow is the result of intense concentration on the present, making us less sensitive to influences that can break the pattern of involvement.

Loss of self–consciousness. As a consequence of the merging described above, awareness of the self disappears. The absence of self-consciousness does not mean that the person is unaware of what is happening in mind or body, but rather that the focus is exclusively on the activity. Wicklund (1986) makes a distinction between subjective and objective self-consciousness that serves to explain this further. When we are objective self-conscious, attention is focused on our thoughts and feelings. This type of self-consciousness does not give in for the flow state. When subjective self-conscious however, attention is centered on the situation and the task we are working on. This type of self-consciousness induces flow.

Time transformation. Flow causes the perception of time to alter. We are used to think of time in sense of past, present and future. In most of our manners, we have a conscious feeling of our actions being related to what is to come and what has been. In flow however, this conscious sense of time becomes distorted, as we no longer consider other time aspects than the one being present, continuously progressing without any reasoning of before and after.

Autotelic experience. The last and ninth element that characterizes flow is what Csikszentmihalyi (1975a) has termed an autotelic experience. This means that flow is intrinsically rewarding. Because flow function as positive reinforcement, it motivates us to work with a task only for the sake of the experience it provides. Csikszentmihalyi describes this as the end result of being in flow.

The nine characteristics of flow presented above serves to provide general characteristics for the understanding of the flow state. However, in order to really understand the complexity of psychological flow and how it can be applied to organizational psychology, a more comprehensive definition is needed. Accordingly, the present thesis suggests that Eckblad's

(1981) scheme theory and Locke and Latham's (1990, 2002) goal setting theory may be used complementary.

1.3.2 Conceptualizing flow through scheme theory

Eckblad (1981) has suggested a somewhat different and more sophisticated conceptualization of flow, primarily inspired by process-oriented views associated with the philosophy of constructive alternativism. This view holds that the organism is a system where one major integrated process is continuously operative. Integrated in this continuous process occurs the flow state, depending on what actions the organism undertake. According to Eckblad (1981), the conceptual independence of cognitive and motivational processes that characterizes present-day psychology fails to give a correct picture of how the mind works. In an attempt to integrate these processes into a unifying theory of psychological flow, Eckblad uses scheme theory to gain the depth lacking in the previous description of flow. As argued by Vitterso, Vorkinn and Vistad, "Eckblad's flow theory is an integration of plans, goals and representations into a dynamic theory of optimal experiences" (2001, p. 140).

The terms associated with scheme theory are primarily adopted from the Piagetian tradition (Eckblad, 1981). The most central concepts of scheme theory will be defined in order to get a clearer picture of what the theory states. Schemes are seen as organized sequences of mental operations, functioning within a hierarchic system. Systems of schemes are continuously operative, where the particular scheme active will depend on the situation we encounter. Eckblad (1981) describes the structure of the scheme as a means-end structure. This explains that every scheme has a beginning and an end, although they are connected to other schemes. More specifically, "any scheme functions as a means in relation to the goals of subordinate schemes, and at the same time as an end or goal for subordinate schemes" (Eckblad, 1981, p. 28). The structure of a scheme then is in order, yet flexible to all types of behaviors within the organism.

Metaphorically speaking, a scheme resembles a lens structure where two poles or distal points function respectively as the start and end phase of a process. Between the beginning and the end phase, there are several potential routes that can influence purposive behavior, depending on the characteristics of the person and the situation. Specifying the final goal of an action in advance will decrease the number of potential routes. Different schemes may be connected to each other within the hierarchical structure. This implies that one structural unit can have smaller structural units as its parts, and that it also can constitute a unit in a more subordinate structure (Eckblad, 1981). A schematic example of the means-end structure is given below in Figure 2.

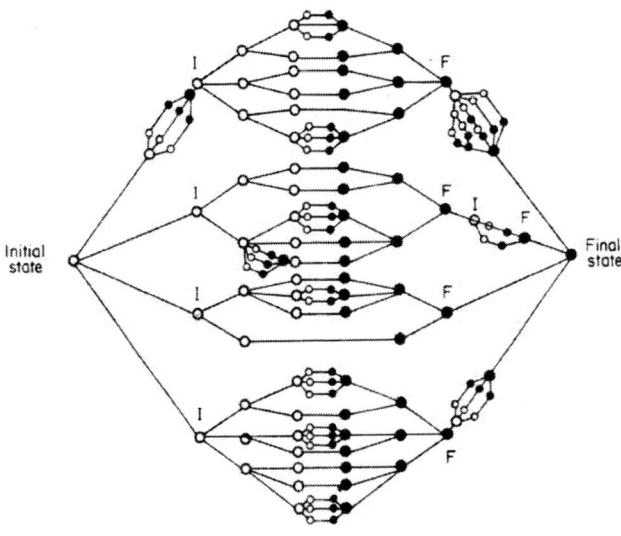

Open circle o = initial state of a scheme (I); Filled circle • = final state of a scheme (F); Corresponding pairs of I and F define schemes. Each scheme corresponds to a path from a o to a •. Pairs nested within a scheme (I – F pair) function vicariously as means or subroutines to that scheme (Eckblad, 1981).

Figure 2. Schematic example of means-end structure.

Schemes, organized in structures resembling the means-end illustration above, are assumed to be responsible for the normal functioning of the individual (Eckblad, 1981). The distal points (I & F) represent a central motivational state and the superior goal, respectively. The mediating paths are descriptions of all possible behavioral outcomes which can occur between the initial and the final state. Only one path is under realization at any one time. The others are latent possibilities that belong to the person's repertoire. An important detail in this theory is that most schemes are never or rarely accessible to awareness (Eckblad, 1998).

Schemes continuously undergo adaptive changes through the processes of assimilation or accommodation. The quality of a feeling state will be determined by the ease of assimilation. Due to the dynamic nature of person-environment interactions, pure assimilation does not exist, thus every event will be somewhat impeded in terms of assimilation (Vittersø, 2004). As an indicator of assimilation ease, Eckblad (1981) has introduced the notion of assimilation resistance (AR). The AR explains degree of discrepancy between an individual's cognitive "map" of a situation and the perception of the "landscape" of the situation. It is the size of this discrepancy that determines the quality of the affective response to the given situation. As described by Vittersø (2003): "The subjective experience advances from easy at very low levels of AR toward pleasant as the AR becomes somewhat larger" (p. 305). Furthermore, these experiences are replaced by affects such as interest and challenge as the AR increase. At very high AR levels, interest and challenge are turned into frustration and anxiety. The more a situation grows complex, the more will the discrepancy grow, ultimately leading to negative affect because the person perceives the situation to be impossible to conceive (Eckblad, 1981; Vittersø, 2004).

When a scheme fails to assimilate it enters a state of disequilibrium. This is a motivational state that causes awareness to center on the activity, driven by the desire to bring the scheme back to the equilibrium state (Eckblad, 1981). The motivational state is a process of accommodation. A scheme can either accommodate through the activation of other sub-schemes, or gradually breed a permanent change where former schemes differentiate into a new version in order to adapt to the new situation. In both cases, there is a continuous process of cognitive and motivational processes where schemes are activated to guide the person through a specific behavior. Shortly stated; when a scheme is in disequilibrium it will attempt to accommodate. According to Eckblad (1981), this is a process of intrinsic motivation which will cause the scheme to become "spontaneously active". Awareness becomes extremely focused; it is perceived as absorbing by the person, and this is what induces the flow experience.

1.3.3 Empirically testing affective responses to assimilation resistance

The quality of an affective response like flow can be assessed using a flow simplex structure (Vittersø, 1998). The term simplex was first defined by Guttmann (1954) as a part of his theory of ordered factors. This theory is an alternative to the better-known theory of common factors. The principle behind a simplex refers to differences in the *degree* between variables belonging to a simple hierarchical organized dimension. The name "simplex" refers to a *sim*ple structure of com*plex*ity between variables of the same dimension (Vittersø et al., 2001). The flow simplex structure draws heavily on the scheme theory and was first defined by Vittersø (1998). As explained above, assimilation resistance is based on a rank order of experiences such as "ease", "pleasant", "joy", "fun", "interest", "challenge", and "dramatic", which means that $E < P < J < F < I < C < D$. Because the positive quality of an affective experience decreases after a peak on "challenges", the rank order is curvilinearly related to

AR. Thus, most statistical methods will fail to reproduce the true structure of these data simply because of the linear arithmetics inherent in these methods (Vitterssø, 2004). This means that the hierarchical structure of a dimension cannot be reproduced by either common factor or principal component analysis. Nevertheless, if the data conform to the pattern of a simplex, it may be detected by inspection of the correlation matrix produced by the simplex variables (Vitterssø, 2004; Vitterssø et al., 2001). This is elaborated in the method section.

1.3.4 Integrating flow in goal setting theory

Pioneered by Locke and his associates, goal setting theory has throughout the years gained widespread acceptance and recognition for its applicability to work performance (Arnold, Cooper, & Robertson, 1998). The core of the theory lies in its guidance to how goals should be generated and assigned, and how it affects behavior. For instance, specifying goals leads to higher performance levels than urging people to do their best (Audia, Kristof-Brown, Brown, & Locke, 1996; Locke & Latham 2002). This is primarily due to the fact that specificity creates a precise intention that helps to shape behavior with precision. If the goals have no external referent, it allows for a wide range of acceptable performance levels. Specific goals involve less ambiguity and clearer coping strategies. Furthermore, research has proven difficult goals to produce the highest levels of effort and performance (Arnold et al., 1998; Kanfer & Ackerman, 1989; Locke & Latham, 2002). A decrease in performance of reaching a difficult goal occurs only when the limits of ability are reached or when commitment to a highly difficult goal lapses (Locke & Latham, 2002).

The most important knowledge we have gained from goal setting research concerns how goals affect work performance. Locke and Latham (2002) recently published a meta-analysis on goal-setting and task motivation. The core findings were summarized to include four different mechanisms in which goals affect performance. First of all, goals direct *attention* and *effort* towards activities that are relevant for reaching the goal, i.e. help the person to focus on strategies that will most efficiently lead him or her towards the completion of a task. Second, goals have an *energizing* function in that high goals lead to greater effort than do low goals. Third, goals affect *endurance* in that high goals prolong effort when participants are allowed to control the time they spend on a task. Forth, there is an indirect affection of *action* in that goals lead to arousal, discovery and use of task-relevant knowledge and strategies (Locke & Latham, 2002). The affects of goals on performance discussed above are moderated by certain factors such as feedback summary, task complexity, commitment, and ability. These will be discussed consecutive in reference to a comparison and contrast analysis between goal-setting theory and the theory of psychological flow.

Comparison and contrast of goal-setting theory and psychological flow. The primary focus of goal-setting theory concerns how a person consciously defines the goals, i.e. the process occurring *prior* to the actual goal reaching behavior. Its attention on the process of reaching a set goal concerns primarily external influences such as feedback and task complexity. The flow theory focuses mainly on the subconscious mental states present as the behavior is carried out.

The aspects of subconscious processes in goal directed behavior merits further attention for at least two reasons. Psychological research frequently divides and fragments human functioning into smaller units for the purpose of mere scientific inquiry. In most cases it is a necessary act because it is impossible to study behavior without conceptualizing its components. However, we rarely attempt to bring the pieces back together again (Abi-Hashem, 2000). Thus, dividing the human mind in conscious and subconscious processes is fruitful for scientific inquiry, but the processes cannot be reduced to two exclusive aspects of behavior. Hence, the attempt of unifying the theories on goal setting and psychological flow can provide a more subtle delineation of work performance.

Secondly, goal-setting theory aims at the work field. When we seek to reveal what behavioral strategies that will increase work performance, it would be most practical to start working on the elements that occur naturally in all humans. Flow is one such element. Every one of us experience flow, it is a highly integrated function of our every-day life. Integrating the knowledge we have on flow into already existing theoretical foundations of organizational psychology will give a contribution to the field.

Similarities between goal-setting theory and psychological flow. The core of the matter is to show how goal-setting theory and the theory of psychological flow can be used complementarily in order to better understand the dynamics of work behavior. Both theories seek to reveal what behavioral premises that increase work performance, but in slightly different manners. To clarify the link between the two theories, an elaborated description of the similarities is given below.

As previously mentioned, flow is characterized by clearly defined goals throughout the action. These goals can either be defined in advance or developed as a consequence of the involvement in the activity. Notice that the former act of goal setting involves a conscious participation from the person where he or she deliberately defines the goal of the action. This is the type of goal setting referred to in goal setting theory (Arnold et al., 1998; Locke, 1997; Locke & Latham, 2002). The latter act of goal setting concerns the subconscious, unintentional goal setting, which develops continuously as a side effect of being in flow. A superior goal often consists of smaller, lower-level goals that serve as a guide for how to reach the final superior goal. These are not necessarily defined in advance; they emerge as a consequence of the different routes taken in the lens structure described by Eckblad (1981).

A match between challenges and skills is one of the most important conditions that need to be present in order to generate flow. Additionally, flow increases performance as a deep concentration on the task is achieved. If the person acting perceive his assignment to be either too difficult or too easy, it is less likely that the performance will generate flow. The same principle applies to goal setting theory, especially when the task is too hard. As argued by Locke and Latham (2002), "performance decreased [only] when the limits of ability were reached" (p. 706, brackets added). Now, why does performance decrease when the skills come too short? It is likely to believe that performance decrease primarily because the person loses his flow. Reaching the limits of ability is a characteristic factor that makes the flow experience fade away.

One of the most consistent findings in goal setting theory is that difficult goals produce the highest levels of effort and performance (Arnold et al., 1998; Locke & Latham, 2002; Kanfer & Ackerman, 1989). The term difficult is a bit inaccurate, and most research articles do not specify what is meant by difficult. Yet, what is defined as difficult would most likely depend on the skills of the person that encounter the goal setting situation. This can be paralleled with the flow theory. The flow model states that the challenges of the task need to be slightly above the level of skills in order to enter and sustain the flow experience (LeFevre, 1992). Challenges in flow resemble the level of difficulty discussed in goal setting theory. If difficult goals are supposed to increase high performance levels, the level of difficulty needs to be slightly above the skills of the person. Otherwise it would not be difficult. This is a clear indication of how goal setting theory and flow can function complementarily, as the challenge-skill dimension is equally important in both theories.

The match between skills and challenges also resembles the depiction of task complexity in goal-setting theory. Task complexity has an important function in the generation of goal setting actions and performance. Personal skills need to resemble the demands inherent in the task. If the complexity of the task increases without corresponding levels of skills, goal effects are dependent on the ability to discover appropriate task strategies (Locke & Latham, 2002). Behavioral consequences of task strategies will be discussed later in the text.

In order for goals to generate the effects on performance discussed above, people need summary feedback that communicates progress in relation to their goals (Arnold et al., 1998; Locke, 1997; Locke & Latham, 2002). Feedback functions as a moderator of goal effects in that the effects become stronger. When appraising work performance, there are at least two different kinds of feedback; namely the external feedback given by others, and the internal, immediate feedback occurring mentally within the actor.

The feedback discussed in goal-setting theory refers to the external type given by others. This type of feedback is usually termed as instructive feedback (Locke, 1997). It provides knowledge of results or progress, thus giving clues on how the person can adjust the goal directed behavior. In one of his articles, Locke (1997) briefly discusses the consequences of not giving instructive feedback. He argues that in the absence of such information, "people have to rely on subjective judgments of the adequacy of their progress, and these are often inaccurate" (Locke, 1997, p. 384). Unfortunately, no references are given on this statement, and this variable has not been included in analyses of goal-setting theory. Of course, in some cases this is a possible consequence. Yet, it could be argued that inaccurate judgments are more likely to occur when goal-reaching behavior fails to induce flow. In flow, the person knows intuitively what the next step of action is; it does not demand a conscious appraisal (Jackson & Marsh, 1996). This internal immediate feedback is a strong indicator of flow and operates continuously as the person acting works his way towards the definite goal. If this internal feedback ceases, flow is interrupted. However, by "subjective judgments" it is likely to believe that Locke describes a conscious appraisal by the person acting, and not the internal feedback seen in flow.

Feedback is also central for the emotional effect of goal reaching behavior, namely satisfaction. According to Locke and Latham (2002), goals serve as a reference standard for satisfaction versus dissatisfaction. Their point is very clearly stated in their recently published meta-analysis: "For any given trial, exceeding the goal provides increasing satisfaction as the positive discrepancy grows, and not reaching the goal creates increasing dissatisfaction as the negative discrepancy grows. Across trials, the more goal successes one has, the higher one's total satisfaction" (Locke & Latham, 2002, p. 709). The authors address primarily the satisfaction experienced through a *conscious* cogitation that occurs either in between or after a goal reaching action. However, it is highly possible to experience a satisfactory feeling when doing something without really being *consciously* aware of that feeling. Flow is often referred to as a highly pleasurable experience, and flow is the positive consequence of directing attention toward a limited sphere of behavioral strategies (Csikszentmihalyi & Csikszentmihalyi, 1992). In other words, flow generates satisfaction (Han 1992; Kowal & Fortier, 1999). Accordingly, goal-reaching behavior contains two dimensions of satisfaction. The first dimension is the one occurring cognitively either in between or after a goal reaching action, discussed in goal setting theory. The other dimension is the satisfaction occurring without conscious appraisal, seen in flow. The immediate and always-present feeling of satisfaction in flow is manifested through the feeling of success in progressing towards the final goal.

It can be questioned to what extent it is necessary to distinguish between the two dimensions of satisfaction. However, both are operative whenever goals generate behavior that breeds a deep concentration of psychic energy. Being aware of this distinction can thus contribute to a more thorough understanding of the mental processes that lead to high work performance. Goal-setting theory fails to explain *why* reaching goals provide increased satisfaction. Hence, flow can be used complementarily.

The flow components of goal-setting behavior. As shown, goal-setting theory encompasses important and useful knowledge that can be used to understand and improve work performance. Yet, one question remains to be answered. What exactly happens sub-consciously when defining goals? What mental phenomena contribute to sustain the goal-reaching motivation? Consider the four mechanisms given above in which goal setting affects performance, i.e. affecting attention, energy, endurance and discovery of task-relevant knowledge. It is suggested that they affect performance because all these mechanisms represent components that enable people to enter and sustain the flow state. Firstly, goals direct attention, which is one of the most important elements of flow. Goals force the attention to be focused on a limited area of stimuli, enabling the person to grow into a deep concentration resembling that of flow. Secondly, we saw that goals also have an energizing function in that it leads to greater effort. However, the energizing function is only present as long as the flow state is operative. If an external factor distracts the attention away from the goal reaching action, they no longer have an energizing function, at least not until attention again is focused on reaching the goal.

The third mechanism stated that goals affect endurance in that high goals prolong effort. Now, why is endurance a consequence of goal setting? Goal setting enables the person to invest his psychic energy in a limited set of behavioral strategies, namely those that will lead to reaching the set goal. Several informants in flow research have explained that the flow state increases the endurance of behavior because they were able to concentrate their psychic energy in the task at hand (Massimini, Delle Fave & Csikszentmihalyi, 1992).

The fourth mechanism described by Locke and Latham (2002) states that goals have an indirect affection of action in that they lead to arousal, discovery and use of task-relevant knowledge and strategies. The theory does not explain the mental processes through which this discovery is possible. The following explanation is suggested: If a person can discover and use task-relevant knowledge and strategies, it implies that this knowledge already exists in the mind but has not been available to consciousness until the knowledge is activated by the goal. In relation to Eckblad's (1981) scheme theory, the discovery of task-relevant strategies will depend on the particular scheme activated. Recall that schemes are seen as organized sequences of mental operations, functioning within a hierarchic system. This hierarchic system consists of smaller units of schemes continuously operative, and the particular scheme active will depend on the situation we encounter. Bear in mind that every scheme is in order, yet flexible to all types of behavior. The behavior of defining a goal will limit the potential routes a scheme can take within the means-end structure. Hence, the person is more likely to make use of task-relevant strategies because the possible routes through the means-end structure are limited. Shortly stated, the routes to irrelevant task strategies are ruled out. This leads us to the suggestion that goals indirectly affect the discovery of task-relevant strategies because it activates the schemes relevant to reach the set goal.

The major difference between goal-setting theory and flow. The major difference between goal setting and flow is the treatment of and the focus on consciousness. Flow focuses primarily on the mental processes occurring subconsciously when a person is absorbed in solving a task. Goal-setting theory in general focuses primarily on how goals are consciously defined in advance of the goal reaching actions. It further elaborates on mediating and moderating effects such as attention, effort, persistence, and feedback, commitment and monetary incentives, respectively. In other words, goal setting theory does not take into account the subconscious processes that is operative during the goal setting and goal reaching actions. As argued by Locke, "… a plausible experimental strategy is to identify the *conscious* mental contents and processes that most directly regulate such action (i.e. goal setting) (1997, p. 377, italics added).

Still, the goal-setting theory is very inclusive and does not necessarily suffer the lack of focus on subconscious processes. However, the theory has undoubtedly a potential of being enriched. Locke does in fact argue that the limitation of the goal-setting model is that it "focuses on conscious motivation and omits the subconscious" (Locke, 1997, p. 404). Furthermore, he states that although the model includes a variety of theoretical perspectives and explains both performance and affect, much more has to be done; "especially on the role of needs, *the effects of subconscious on action*, and the integration of the various theories with each other" (Locke, 1997, p. 404, italics added).

What distinguishes the two then, is that flow both has a definite goal and continuous goals inherent when it is operative. Goal-setting theory in general focuses only on the definite goal, and not the mental processes through which it is gained. How we see this distinction depends on how we choose to define goals. Goal-setting theory defines goals as being the object or aim of an action. Specifically, a consciously held goal is the end the person wants to achieve (Locke, 1997). On the other hand, goals can also be defined as means through which we seek a pleasurable state. As Csikszentmihalyi puts it, "goals are really means; they are pursued in order to achieve a positive affective state. A pianist does not play in order to finish the piece as quickly as possible; the goal of completing the piece is simply the means by which the pianist can experience the enjoyment of playing" (Csikszentmihalyi & Nakamura, 1999, p. 108).

Either of the two definitions is applicable, depending on the characteristics of the situation we encounter, i.e. the circumstances in which the goals are set. The pianist given as an example above can set a superior goal, which is to learn how to play a given piece by heart. This type of goal setting resembles the one defined by goal setting theory. On the other hand, the reason why that goal was set in the first place is because it functions as a means through which the pianist can gain the flowing pleasurable feeling of playing the piano. The piece will provide a deeper flow if the pianist knows it by heart. Lacking the knowledge of what chord to play next will interrupt the flow state. Consequently, goal setting becomes an instrument through which flow can be obtained. Very often, behavior that initially is motivated by external factors can turn into a behavior motivated by the desire to experience the pleasurable feeling it provides. There is no longer a distinction between what must be done and what one wishes to do (Csikszentmihalyi & Csikszentmihalyi, 1999).

By now, a short sum-up is needed to keep the red line straight. Based on the comparison and contrast analysis given above, the following statement is interesting for scientific scrutiny: Goal setting may increase the occurrence of flow, provided that the rules for productive goal setting are followed. Specific goals help attention to be centered on the task at hand, which is an important condition of flow. Difficult goals may function as an indicator of the challenges that Csikszentmihalyi assumes to regulate the intensity of the flow experience. Furthermore, goals may function as a reference standard that provides feedback to the person on his or her performance, serving to sustain the flow state. This leads to the hypothesis that those high on personal goal setting will experience more flow.

1.4 Towards a unified theory of flow in organizational psychology

One of the major challenges faced by contemporary psychology is to overcome the boundaries that exist between different theoretical disciplines. To fully understand the complexity of the working mind, it is necessary to bring the pieces of discoveries back together (Abi-Hasem, 2000). Moreover, we should continue revising already existing theories as new potential contributions are being made. As shown by the theoretical analysis given in the previous section, Csikszentmihalyi's flow theory has a potential of being enriched, as do the theory of goal setting by Locke and Latham.

Recall that the nine characteristics given by Csikszentmihalyi and his associates were challenge-skill balance, clear goals, unambiguous feedback, sense of control, action-awareness merging, concentration on task at hand, loss of self-consciousness, transformation of time, and that the experience is autotelic. First of all, it is interesting to investigate whether all nine dimensions are equally important to the flow experience in work settings as they have proven to be in sports settings. For the purpose of clarity, these characteristics can also be divided into three major dimensions. These are prerequisites of flow, immediate experiential characteristics of flow, and subsequent consequences of flow. This is especially convenient when including other theoretical contributions such as scheme theory and goal setting theory. Mark however that this distinction is for theoretical purpose only and will not be tested empirically, as none of the flow measurements applied in the present study are built on such a distinction.

1.4.1 Prerequisites of flow

In one of his writings, Csikszentmihalyi introduces the challenge-skill dimension by saying: "It is easier to become completely involved in a task if we believe it is doable. If it appears to be beyond our capacity we tend to respond to it by feeling anxious; if the task is too easy we get bored" (Csikszentmihalyi, 2003, p. 44). This implies that we consciously appraise the situation prior to a potential flow-inducing activity. Thus, the challenge-skill dimension could be defined a prerequisite of flow because it decides whether the flow experience will occur or not. Since Csikszentmihalyi includes the challenge-skill dimension as a characteristic of the flow experience, it is unclear whether he would define this dimension as a prerequisite or an immediate consequence of the flow state. However, a perception of the challenge-skill dimension cannot exclusively be an immediate experiential consequence of flow if it has not been a prerequisite in advance. This means that a match between challenges and skills cannot develop out of the involvement with the activity if the personal and situational factors prior to a flow experience do not allow it. Perception of a challenge-skill balance would necessarily have to be present throughout a flow-activity in order to sustain the experience, but it nevertheless sets the standards prior to entering flow.

The clear goal dimension is another characteristic of flow that fits in to a prerequisite dimension. As seen in the nine characteristics specified by Csikszentmihalyi (1992, 1997, 2003) and Jackson and Marsh (1996), clear goals emerge as a consequence of the involvement in the task. Csikszentmihalyi (2003) points out that the ultimate goal of an action is important, but that it more often *interferes* with performance. He explains that people often miss the opportunity to enjoy what they do because they focus all their attention on the outcome, rather than savoring the steps along the way. Unfortunately, no research references are given as support for this statement. Both Eckblad's scheme theory and Locke and Latham's goal setting theory actually proves the contrary. Csikszentmihalyi does outline that the primary concern in his description of flow is "the quality of the experience *during* performance", and not what constitutes a successful performance (Csikszentmihalyi, 2003, p. 43). Yet, as shown by now, decisions made prior to an action may affect both duration and intensity of flow. For instance, specific and high goals increase the likelihood of discovering task related coping strategies (Locke & Latham, 2002). This will limit potential routes taken in the lens structure, thus leading to a merging of goals and the plan to reach those goals (Eckblad, 1981). Consequently, it is suggested that the clear goal dimension is better defined as a prerequisite of flow, although goals also may develop along the activity.

The bottom line is that both these dimensions, i.e. challenge – skill and clear goals, need to continuously adapt throughout the activity in order to sustain the flow state, but it is only possible to do so if they have been present in advance.

1.4.2 Immediate experiential characteristics of flow

Time alteration, loss of self-consciousness, action-awareness merging, concentration on task at hand, sense of control, and immediate feedback are all experiential characteristics of flow (Csikszentmihalyi & Csikszentmihalyi, 1992; Csikszentmihalyi 1997, 2003; Jackson & Marsh, 1996). All these characteristics are limited to exist only in the presence of flow, and would thus naturally fit into a category meant to describe only the immediate experiential characteristics of the state. Based on the contributions made earlier, Eckblad's (1981) scheme theory may further explain some of these characteristics, namely the action-awareness merging and the sense of control dimension.

Recall that the merging dimension explains what we experience as a total absorption in flow. Attention must be totally preoccupied by the current activity and behavior flows more or less intuitively (Vitterrsø et al., 2001). What is missing from this description is the reason *why* the flow state is perceived like this. Eckblad's scheme theory may fill the gaps. When one defines a goal, there exists an affective discrepancy between the present situation and the desired situation. According to Eckblad (1981), the affective quality of how this discrepancy is perceived is determined by assimilation resistance (AR). Bear in mind that high levels of AR is perceived as challenging yet positive, whereas too high levels breeds frustration and agonize. However, discrepancy centre attention, and if there is a solution to the problem, a scheme becomes spontaneously active and the person enters flow. In such situations, means and goals are not represented as separate entities in awareness, thus attention will not be divided between them (Eckblad, 1981; Vitterssø, 2004). The merging of goals with their plans is what happens when a scheme becomes spontaneously active and the person enters flow (Eckblad, 1981). This serves to explain why flow is perceived so absorbing; the person is intrinsically motivated because the activity itself becomes the goal. Hence, Eckblad's scheme theory may explain why the flow is perceived to be so absorbing.

Assimilation resistance may also explain the sense of control, conveyed through an immediate feedback. When the AR is low, the person is left feeling at ease. When AR is high however, yet not beyond the capacity of what is manageable, schemes will linger in a motivational state that makes them spontaneously active. Although not accessible to awareness, these mechanisms breed a feeling of coping and may be an explanation to why flow leaves us feeling in control of our actions.

1.4.3 Subsequent consequences of flow

As argued by Csikszentmihalyi and Csikszentmihalyi (1992), although not specified as distinct from other characteristics, the autotelic experience is the end result of being in flow. Because it is an effect registered by the actor after the actual experience, it is more clearly described as a subsequent consequence of being in flow. Again, this distinction is not made for the purpose of empirical analysis, but theoretically by means of making the theory more easily presented.

By now, a unified theory of flow in organizational psychology has been presented, primarily based on the work of Csikszentmihalyi, Eckblad, Locke and Latham. The main aim of the present thesis is to build a theoretical foundation on which a flow model may facilitate our understanding of work behavior. Based on this theoretical foundation, the relation between flow and goal setting, work motivation, work performance, and job satisfaction will be empirically tested. Prior to this, a theoretical analysis of how flow relates to these work behavioral aspects will be presented.

1.5 Theoretical foundation for work motivation, work performance and job satisfaction
1.5.1 Psychological flow and work motivation
Work motivation is presently understood as the degree to which an employee is self-motivated to perform effectively. Motivation is thus defined by the extent to which a person

experiences positive feelings when doing well and negative reactions when working poorly (Hackman & Oldham, 1975). Several interview research studies have shown that flow leaves the person feeling motivated to continue engaging in the given flow-activity. Most of these findings however are made in sport activities, leisure, and educational settings, as research primarily has focused on these aspects (Csikszentmihalyi, 2003; Jackson & Marsh, 1996; Kowal & Fortier, 1999; Larson, 1992). One research study conducted by Csikszentmihalyi and LeFevre (1989) investigated flow and motivation in work and leisure settings. They found that motivation responses were three times higher in leisure activities than in work settings. However, motivation was measured with one item asking respondents if they wish they were doing something else, which might not be an accurate measure of work motivation. In one of his recent books, Csikszentmihalyi (2003) argues that flow is motivating in work settings. This statement is based on the interviews of several business employees, most of whom were executive leaders. However, he does not refer to any empirical analyses that report general tendencies of correspondences between flow and work motivation. Thus, it is necessary to investigate this phenomenon among employees in different occupations.

The flow experience is motivating in two manners. Firstly, flow provides an immediate and continuous motivation to fulfill the task at hand. Perceived control, total involvement, and balance of challenges and skills constitute an inspiration to continue. Secondly, flow function as positive reinforcement. According to general principles of learning psychology, this will motivate the person to seek the same tasks over again because he or she has learned what motivating effects the experience had (Marr, 2001). In both instances, behavior is driven by intrinsic motivation, i.e. without any reward other than the one provided by the activity itself.

Psychology has a tradition of distinguishing between intrinsic and extrinsic motivation. Several studies show that adding external rewards reduce, and in some cases even eliminate, the initial internal motivation. If so be it, stimulating employees to work by means of internal motivation would be impossible because the work domain is mainly based on the principle of external rewards. Yet, Cameron, Banko and Pierce (2001) conducted a meta analysis on existing research results, which concluded that the empirical basis of the motivation theory was not sufficient to sustain the conclusion. The interactive effect of both types of motivation would probably serve to explain work motivation in a better way. Porter and Lawler (1968) have argued that optimal work performance occurs when there is a combination of intrinsic motivating work tasks and external rewards are added.

Kowal and Fortier (1999) discuss the ambiguous findings on the relation between internal and external motivation and psychological flow. He refers to Csikszentmihalyi and LeFevre's (1989) findings of positive correlations between intrinsic motivation and flow. Contrary, Mannell, Zuzanek and Larson (1988, in Kowal & Fortier, 1999) found that flow frequency increased with external motivating rewards. Still others have found that both types of motivation are clearly related to flow (e. g. Hills, Argyle & Reeves, 2000).

An important aim of the present paper is to investigate whether flow experiences lead to increased levels of work motivation. Most research projects on flow and motivation have proven intrinsic motivation to be the primary motivational effect of flow. Furthermore, since this study investigates the effects flow has on motivation, and not the other way around, an interesting research question would be that flow increases intrinsic motivation in work settings.

1.5.2 Psychological flow and job satisfaction

Job satisfaction is presently defined as a general feeling an employee has towards his or her job. People who experience flow regularly report feeling more satisfied, more in control, and less dependent on external rewards (Han, 1992; Kowal & Fortier, 1999). Satisfaction is manifested at two levels. First of all, the flow experience is often described as intensely pleasurable (Csikszentmihalyi & Csikszentmihalyi, 1992). This may be due to the fact that flow involves a level of concentration that does not leave room for worrying or distractions. Thus, the flow state creates an off-zone for irrelevant thoughts and emotional discomfort. Secondly, aggregated experiences of satisfaction will in turn create a general sense of satisfaction. In fact, research has shown that flow deprivation causes tense and irritable mood, anxiety and symptoms of depression (Csikszentmihalyi, 1996). The flow experiences studied above are presumably no different from the kind of flow people experience at work. Thus, it makes sense to assume that high levels of flow in work settings will lead to high levels of satisfaction at work.

1.5.3 Psychological flow and work performance

Work performance as a concept covers a wide range of behavioral incentives. Production records, absenteeism, disciplinary, hours spent at work and lateness are just a few examples of how to objectively appraise the employees' performance. In the present thesis, the *subjective experience* of flow is the main focus. Accordingly, the employee's subjective experience of his or her own work performance in relation to flow is of main interest.

Jackson and Marsh (2001) investigated the relation between flow and optimal performance in sports activities. They found that two of the nine flow dimensions, i.e. autotelic experience and challenge-skill balance was significantly related to the overall performance of an event. To the knowledge of the author, no research studies have yet empirically tested the effect of flow on work performance. However, this is an interesting research inquiry because working on a task that generates the flow state increases the cognitive efficacy (Marr, 2001). Flow is focused attention, and focused attention implies that all psychic energy is invested in the task at hand (Csikszentmihalyi & Csikszentmihalyi, 1992). Thus, it makes sense to assume that employees would appraise their own performance as being better when in flow, as opposed to being bored, anxious or in apathy.

1.6 Aims of the thesis

By now, a theoretical basement for introducing flow to organizational psychology has been made, which is an important aim of this thesis. As far as known by now, the link between goal setting, flow and work related factors have not yet been tested empirically. It was therefore necessary to build up a theoretical framework that represents a solid basement for statistical analysis. Empirically speaking, the primary aim of the thesis is to investigate if and how we can use flow as a resource. This aim is based on the idea that goal setting may increase flow, and that flow may increase work motivation, work performance, and job satisfaction. The specific hypotheses of the master thesis are presented as specific aims of paper 1 and 2, respectively.

1.6.1 Specific aims of 1st article

1. The first paper used the Flow State Scale (FSS) to measure flow in work settings. This scale was originally developed to measure flow in sports activities (Jackson & Marsh, 1996). In an attempt to make the FSS fit to measure flow in work setting, some of the items were rewritten prior to the data collection process. Consequently, dimensionality, reliability, internal consistency, and discriminant validity of the revised version need to be tested. Furthermore, it is interesting to investigate whether all nine dimensions of the FSS are equally important to work settings as they are to sports activities.

2. Based on previous findings in sport and physical activity studies, research has shown that flow increases motivation. Accordingly, it is hypothesized that flow increases employees' experience of work motivation. Because flow is experienced as satisfactory, satisfaction is assumed to function as a complementary predictor of work motivation.
3. Based on the theoretical analysis of goal setting and flow given above, the third aim of the first article is to investigate the effects of goal setting on flow. It is hypothesized that the act of goal setting will contribute to increased levels of the flow experience.

1.6.2 Specific aims of 2nd article

1. The first research aim of the second article is to investigate whether the data confirm to the flow simplex structure, furthermore enabling the specific hypotheses of the second article to be tested in relation to a simplex structure of flow.
2. The first flow-simplex situation in the questionnaire asked respondents to recall an incident of being totally absorbed in the task at hand. It is hypothesized that this situation is representative for the flow state, i.e. that it is perceived as fun, interesting and challenging. Furthermore, such a situation is believed to increase the employees' motivation, satisfaction and work performance, both while in the flow state, and after the flow state has occurred.
3. The second flow-simplex situation considered the experience of not having enough time to finish a task. Respondents were asked to think of a situation in which they felt really stressed out on time yet had to finish the task at hand. No theoretical foundation exists to hypothesize how such a situation is perceived in relation to the flow structure, work motivation, work performance and job satisfaction. Consequently, it is generally interesting to gain information about how this situation will turn out.
4. The third situation asked respondents to think of a situation in which they had plenty of time to finish the task at hand. Missing theoretical foundation for specification of hypothesis applies for this situation as well. Accordingly, empirical analyses aims at exploring how such a situation relates to the flow-simplex variables, work motivation, work performance, and job satisfaction.
5. The fourth situation concerned not succeeding in reaching an important goal of a work task. The primary interest was to investigate how such a situation relates to the flow-simplex variables and work performance, work motivation, and job satisfaction.

6. The next specific aims of the second article are to investigate the subsequent effects of the four situations. It is hypothesized that the flow situation will be the most important experience in relation to high levels of work performance, work motivation, and job satisfaction.

2.0 Method

2.1 Sample

Data were collected through a self-completing questionnaire survey. The sample consisted of 170 employees at 9 different organizations in Norway, 78 were women and 91 were men. One participant did not specify gender. Average age of the group was 38 years (SD = 9.0), 54 % had university education, and 96 % worked full time.

The sample represented occupations from technology, financial departments, medical business, social services, and salesmen. Initially, 12 different organizations were invited to participate in the present study. All organizations were selected from the list of customers of a consulting company in the Municipality of Trondheim. The executives in daily charge of each workplace were invited to include their employees in the study. Nine of these agreed to distribute the questionnaires to their employees. All the attendants were informed in advance that the data would be treated confidentially. Of the 400 questionnaires distributed, 170 were returned, which gives a response rate of 42,5 %.

2.2 Procedure

The executives in daily charge of each workplace were invited to include their employees in the study, and gave their approval for the distribution of questionnaires to the potential respondents, i.e. the employees. The questionnaires were returned in an envelope located at each workplace to make sure that the data collection process sustained anonymous.

2.3 Questionnaire

The questionnaire consisted of two parts. The first part measured general occurrences of psychological flow, work motivation, job satisfaction, work performance, and goal setting. The second part measured the flow experience in specific situations, where respondent were asked to recall four different types of situations and then grade their flow experience on a flow simplex structure. This part of the questionnaire also contained items on motivation, satisfaction and work performance related to the specific flow instance.

Demographic and Work Characteristics. Personal demographic variables included year of birth, gender, marital status, and education. Work characteristics included the present work situation, number of years engaged in the occupation, tenure in the present position, work hours during a week, and overtime hours during a week.

2.3.1 General part of the questionnaire

Flow State Scale. A nine-dimensional scale consisting of 36 items was used to measure level and intensity of the flow experience in general. Flow was assessed on a 5-point Likert-type scale ranging from strongly disagree to strongly agree. The scale was originally developed and validated by Jackson and Marsh (1996) to measure flow in sport and physical activity settings. However, in order to fit the scale to work settings, some of the items had to be revised.

The questionnaire was initially translated into Norwegian by three individual translators, and then translated back to English by different persons in order to discover potential discrepancies. Some of the items were revised in order to suit a work situation instead of a sport situation. The original form of the questionnaire was kept, making only minor adjustments to fit the work situation. The final version was worked out in a discussion group using all available suggestions. Before responding to the flow state scale, respondents were asked to recall a specific situation at work where they experienced being totally absorbed in a task. In order to keep in mind the flow experience while responding to the items, respondents were asked to write down the situation they were thinking of.

Work motivation. A scale developed and validated by Lawler and Hall (1970) was used to assess work motivation. The scale consists of four items graded on a 5-point Likert-type scale ranging from strongly disagree to strongly agree.

Job satisfaction. A three-item scale developed and validated by Hackman and Oldman (1975) assessed job satisfaction. The items were graded on a 5-point Likert-type scale ranging from strongly disagree to strongly agree.

Work performance. Respondents gave a subjective appraisal of perceived work performance. Evaluation scale was a 5-point Likert-type ranging from "very poorly" to "very good". Prior to this rating, the subjects were asked to write down the five most important work tasks that characterized their job in order to make a more accurate appraisal.

Goal-setting. A two-dimensional scale consisting of nine items was used to measure personal goal setting and organizational goals. All the items were based on a systematic theoretical inquiry of Locke and Latham's (1990) goal setting theory, most of which were selected from their own questionnaire. The original questionnaire by Locke and Latham consisted of 54 items, which was too comprehensive to include in the present study.

2.3.2 Specific part of the questionnaire

Flow simplex structure. The flow simplex structure developed by Vittersø (1998) was used to assess flow in specific situations. The flow simplex measurement is made up of seven adjectives that characterize the flow state. The adjectives are presented on a bipolar semantic differential scale, and subjects responded to a seven-point scale listed between the binary adjectives. Although unipolar scales have proven to conform to the notion of a flow-simplex as well, the bipolar format was chosen to keep the model in line with Eckblad's initial work (Vittersø, 2004). The flow adjectives were easy-difficult, pleasant-unpleasant, joyful-sad, fun-boring, interesting-uninteresting, challenging-tame, and dramatic-undramatic. A more detailed description of the theoretical foundation for the flow simplex structure is presented in the second article of the thesis, which uses this method to analyze flow in specific situations.

Four specific situations were assessed using the flow simplex structure. These were (1) being totally absorbed and engaged in a task, (2) being very short on time to finish a task, (3) having plenty of time to finish a task, and (4) not succeeding in reaching a set goal. Respondents were asked to recall an instance of the given situation, and write down this situation in provided areas. After responding to the flow simplex structure following the given specific situation, four items measuring work performance, work motivation and job satisfaction followed. The entire questionnaire is presented in appendix B.

2.4 Statistical analyses

In the first article, Principal Component Analysis with iteration and varimax rotation was applied on all measurement questionnaires to detect the underlying dimensions of the variables. Structural Equation Modelling Made Simple (STREAMS) offers a consistent interface to the LISREL program and was used to test the fit of the flow models found in the exploratory factor analysis (Gustafsson & Stahl, 2000; Jørskog & Sørbom, 1993). Chronbach's alpha coefficient evaluated the internal consistency of the indices. Average total inter item correlations were also calculated, and correlation analysis was used to measure discriminant validity. Stepwise regression analyses and hierarchical block regression analyses were carried out to test the relationship between flow, work motivation and goal setting.

Principal Component Analysis using a chain P-technique was executed to unfold the data of the flow simplex. Group mean differences of factor scores for employees high and low in the variables work performance, work motivation, and job satisfaction were examined by means of t-tests. Multivariate analysis of variance (MANOVA) was applied to analyze differences between the flow dimensions defined by Csikszentmihalyi and demographic variable. MANOVA was also used to measure whether or not there were an overall effect of the four situations on work performance, work motivation, and job satisfaction. One-way analysis of variance (ANOVA) tested each of the dependent variables work performance, work motivation, and job satisfaction in relation to the four situations.

3.0 Results
3.1 Main results of 1st article

The core aim of the first article was to test the dimensionality, reliability, internal consistency, and discriminant validity of the revised version of Flow State Scale (FSS). Based on the new version of the FSS, associations between goal setting, flow, and work motivation was investigated. The results of the factor analyses indicated that an eight-dimensional structure of flow may suit data collection in work settings better than the original nine-dimensional structure, although the differences were small. Furthermore, only two of the flow dimensions were significantly related both to work motivation and goal setting, i.e. the clear goal dimension and the autotelic dimension. The same two flow dimensions were significantly related to goal setting, indicating that these two are the most important characteristics of flow in work settings. Based on the theoretical analysis given introductory and the results of the empirical analyses, it is suggested that goal setting may be a functional technique applicable to increase levels of flow in work settings. Furthermore, increased levels of flow may contribute to increased levels of work motivation. However, future research should try to replicate these findings using a better measurement of goal setting than the one applied presently.

3.2 Main results of 2nd article

The flow simplex structure was tested in four specific work situations, i.e. (1) being totally absorbed in the task at hand (flow), (2) not having enough time to finish a task, (3) having plenty of time to finish a task, and (4) not succeeding in reaching a set goal. The flow simplex structure unfolded by the present data was investigated in these four situations in relation to the employees' subjective experience of work performance, work motivation, and job satisfaction. It was further hypothesized that the flow situation would increase work performance, work motivation, and job satisfaction. Results indicated that flow in work settings is primarily experienced as fun and interesting, whereas research in other domains has found challenges to be an important characteristic of flow. Employees high on work performance, work motivation, and job satisfaction perceives the flow situation to be pleasant, fun, and joyful, respectively. Most employees experienced the time pressure situation as uncomfortable and sad, and the plenty of time situation as easy. The unsuccessful situation did not have any adequate relation to the flow simplex adjectives. However, those who nevertheless managed to stay high in work performance perceived the time pressure to be somewhat fun and interesting, whereas the plenty of time situation was perceived as pleasant and joyful and the unsuccessful situation as joyful. Employees high in work motivation experienced both time pressure, plenty of time, and the unsuccessful situation as interesting. Those high in job satisfaction primarily experienced the time pressure situation as fun, the plenty of time situation as a bit more interesting, and the unsuccessful situation to be pleasant. Finally, the flow situation was strongly related to work performance, work motivation, and job satisfaction, indicating that flow may be an important predictor of these work behavior characteristics.

4.0 Discussion and implications

4.1 Measuring the flow experience

Two approaches have been applied to measure flow in the present thesis; the Flow State Scale (FSS) developed by Jackson and Marsh (1996) and the flow simplex structure developed by Eckblad (1980) and further revised by Vittersø (1998). These measurements differ both in theoretical basement, dimensional division, and mathematical logic. However, both measurements aim at explaining affective responses to deep concentration and total absorption. Analysis of dimensionality showed that an eight-dimensional structure of the modified FSS version seemed to suit the present data better than the original nine-dimensional structure suggested by Jackson and Marsh (1996). The comparison analysis between the two showed that the one based on eight dimensions was slightly more sensitive to the variations in work motivation. However, only two of the nine and eight dimensions which constitute the FSS proved to be significantly related to work motivation and goal setting, namely the clear goal and the autotelic dimension. Several explanations may account for these findings. The theoretical distinction of the nine dimensions made introductory suggested that the clear goal dimension should be explained as a prerequisite for flow. This implied that the rules and goals for behavior in a given situation need to be clear in advance, although they also may develop along the activity. If this is correct, one reason why this dimension was significantly related to both work motivation and goal setting may be that it is easier for participants to recall this characteristic when responding to the questionnaire. None of the immediate experiential effects of flow were significant, which may indicate that the subconscious processes of flow are difficult to remember. The autotelic dimension was theorized to belong in subsequent category of flow, which also might have been easier to recall than immediate experiential effects.

There is also a chance that only these two are important in work related flow experiences, and that the remaining seven dimensions only are crucial in sports, educational, and leisure settings. Certain differences between sports activities and work tasks may account for these differences, although a deep concentration characterizes both flow experiences. Sports usually involve more physical motions whereas work relies primarily on cognitive processes. However, research findings are ambiguous in this matter.

Although several factor analyses suggests nine or eight dimensions of flow in the analysis of 36 items (e.g., Jackson & Marsh, 1996; Jackson, Thomas, Marsh, & Smethurst, 2001; Straume, 2004a), it does not necessarily mean that flow should be conceptualized through multiple dimensions. An important theoretical issue stems form the present findings, namely that we need to appraise to what extent it is fruitful to explain flow through as many as nine or eight dimensions. This multidimensional distinction was made some 30 years ago, and it can be debated whether or not this distinction is sufficiently supported through research. The characteristics are indeed functional when describing the flow state, especially as they are derived from almost half a million interviews conducted around the world. However, the current results show that the dimensions are less distinct than initially assumed. The same results were gained by Vittersø and Kjøndahl (2003), who found that the nine dimensional flow construct was not a valid indicator of flow. Consequently, the multidimensional structure might not be suited for empirical analysis of the flow experience. Moreover, a growing body of research results suggests that flow is curvilinearly related to affective responses (e.g., Vitterø, 1998, 2003; Vitterø et al., 2001). Although not articulated, this is implicitly acknowledged by Csikszentmihalyi in his flow-zone Figure (see Figure 1, p. 13). Because of the linear aritmethics inherent in most statistical procedures, this curvilinear relation cannot be accounted for by the FSS.

The flow simplex analysis seems to be more sensitive to a quantitatively based measure of flow in work settings. The mathematical logic behind a simplex structure allows for curvilinear relations between affective responses that are assumed to constitute the flow experience. Both the FSS and the simplex were tested in relation to work motivation on the same sample, and the flow simplex proved to explain a significantly larger amount of work motivation than did the FSS. This may account for the relatively small proportion of variance explained by the FSS dimensions, and indicate that the flow simplex may be a better option to use when empirically testing the flow experience.

Another advantage of the flow simplex is the size of the questionnaire. It consists of only seven adjectives termed on a bipolar semantic differential scale. The original version of the FSS contains 36 items, and requires substantially more time to respond to. One insufficiency however is that the theoretical basis for the flow simplex is largely based on the scheme theory and the subconscious cognitive and motivational processes of behavior, which cannot be directly tested. The flow simplex tests an assumed assimilation resistance parallel to the subjective experiences, and only the latter is directly measured. Although the results showed that flow was significantly related to work performance, work motivation, and job satisfaction, the experience of applying the flow simplex to measure flow in work settings is limited. More research is needed before any conclusions can be drawn.

4.2 Flow experiences at work
Percentage of experienced flow was calculated in the second article, based on the eight-dimensional structure suggested by the factor analyses. The clear goal and the autotelic dimensions gained the highest values, indicating that these were the strongest indicators of

flow. The merging of self and activity, the loss of self-consciousness, and the time alteration were the lowest, all of which belong to the immediate experiential effects of flow. Again, either this may be due to the fact that these characteristics are not as strong in flow experiences at work, or they may be caused by measurement errors.

Csikszentmihalyi's flow theory is strongly based on the notion of a challenge-skill balance. In fact, he argues that this is a necessary condition of flow (e.g., Csikszentmihalyi & Nakamura, 1999). Yet, the flow simplex analyses portrayed the flow experience to be characterized primarily as fun and interesting, and not as challenging as initially expected. The seven variables of the flow simplex represent a rank order of assimilation resistance, and challenges impose a larger gap in the assimilation resistance than fun and interesting. Consequently, the results may signify that flow inducing work tasks are not necessarily challenging. Perhaps it is easier to purposively adjust the level of challenges in sports and leisure settings along with the development of skills. The possibility to adjust the level of challenges at work necessitates that employees are autonomous and free to make decisions about their own work situation. Perhaps the role of autonomy facilitates the flow experience at work. Future studies should aim at investigating the potential relation between the intensity of flow and levels of autonomy.

Accounting for personal emotional experiences can be biased in various ways (Thomas & Diener, 1990). The seemingly low levels of challenges in work flow may be caused by memory biases of self-reporting questionnaires. The act of recalling subjective experiences involves reconstructions (e.g., Singer & Salovey, 1993), and some studies have found that events are remembered more positively than the original experience (Vitterso, personal communication, 24. May, 2004). Yet, the precise nature of memory bias remains to be determined, as other studies conclude differently (see Baumeister, Bratslavsky, & Finkenauer, 2001, for an overview). Nevertheless, a growing body of studies have recognized that affective experiences are reported differently in real-time as compared with in retrospect (e.g., Kahneman, 1999). This effect may account for some of the results reported in the current study.

4.3 The role of goal setting in flow experiences

The hypothesis that goal setting actions may increase the occurrence of flow was partly confirmed in the first article. Goal setting was significantly related to the clear goal and the autotelic dimensions, the same two dimensions that predicted levels of work motivation. Again, it seems as if these two dimensions either are the most important elements of the flow experience in work situations, or that recalling the immediate experiential components of flow was too difficult for the employees. As far as the clear goal dimension is a prerequisite of flow, it resembles the presence of consciously defined goals. It might be easier for respondents to appraise their own flow experience by focusing on factors that are more easily represented in awareness. Low validity of the goal setting measurement may also account for these findings. Goal setting was only assumed to increase flow provided that the rules for productive goal setting were followed. Recall that specific and difficult goals are assumed to increase productive work performance. The present study did not make sure that these rules were followed; neither did it test the degree to which goals were specific or difficult, but rather the general tendency of organizing work tasks through the specification of clear goals. However, prior to the empirical analyses, a thorough evaluation of the possible link between flow and goal setting was made. This evaluation suggested that goal setting and flow have certain similarities and complementary features that may explain work behavior correspondingly. The extensive focus on subconscious processes made it difficult to investigate all aspects of the complementary factors, yet future research should aim at developing new ways of testing this relation empirically.

The second article tested how the act of not reaching a set goal was experienced, as opposed to the tendency of defining goals which was tested in the first article. No specific hypothesis was defined in advance; it was generally interesting to investigate how employees would experience this situation in relation to the flow simplex variables. Relative to the low scorers, those who managed to stay high in work performance, work motivation, and job satisfaction perceived the unsuccessful situation to be interesting, challenging, and pleasant, respectively. This could mean that goal setting still may increase flow experiences even if employees do not succeed in reaching the defined goal, provided that they stay high in work performance, work motivation, and job satisfaction. However, this relation is not directly empirically tested, but nevertheless an interesting research inquiry that should be investigated in future studies.

4.4 Using flow as a resource to increase work motivation, performance and satisfaction
One of the main aims of the current master thesis was to investigate whether the effects of flow would enhance work motivation, work performance, and job satisfaction. The

presentation of previous findings and theoretical interpretations lead to this assumption. The analyses based on the flow simplex structure confirmed this assumption.

4.4.1 Psychological flow and work motivation

The relation between flow and internal work motivation was tested in three different manners. Other studies have found external motivation to be a predictor of flow (Kowal and Fortier, 1999), but the present thesis tested if flow could predict motivation. Flow cannot increase external motivation, almost by definition. Hence, the data collection of the thesis was based on intrinsic motivation only. The first article examined the nine and eight dimensions of flow in relation to work motivation. The fact that only two of the dimensions (clear goal and autotelic experience) explained variance in work motivation indicated that the remaining dimensions were not sensitive to work settings, or that recalling the immediate experiential effects of flow while responding to a questionnaire is too difficult. In fact, most people have never really considered the characteristics of the flow experience, thus complicating the reconstruction process that retrospective items imply.

The next two analyses of motivation and flow regarded how those high in work motivation experienced the process of being in flow, and whether or not high levels of motivation in a specific situation could be explained by the flow experience. Employees high in work motivation perceived the flow situation to be joyful and fun. In fact, the flow situation was experienced as less challenging than the remaining three situations, indicating that degree of assimilation resistance was lowest in this situation. The memory bias discussed above may explain these findings as well, meaning that although flow was experienced as challenging while in the state, subjects remembered it to be joyful and fun. The final analysis showed that flow facilitates work motivation as motivation was significantly stronger in the flow situation compared to the remaining three. Yet, work performance and job satisfaction was even stronger effects of flow at work.

4.4.2 Psychological flow and work performance

The relation between flow and work performance was tested in a specific situation, and employees high in work performance perceived the flow situation to be joyful. Although the results showed that flow clearly was a predictor of work performance, this study alone is not enough to conclude that this is correct. The present study measured the subjective experience of work performance, which implies that respondents appraised and graded their personal experience of their own efficiency in a given situation. It was chosen to use this measure because the work performance was appraised relative to the personal experience of being in flow. Although self-evaluations might be sensitive to the desire of self-enhancements (Festinger, 1954), other studies have concluded that people's ability to evaluate themselves closely corresponds to performance on criterion measures (for an overview, see Mabe & West, 1982). Yet, the effect of flow should also be studied with objective measures of work performance. Furthermore, this relation was presently tested in one specific flow situation, and other studies should try to measure the effects of aggregated flow situations.

4.4.3 Psychological flow and job satisfaction

Two aspects of job satisfaction were tested in the present study. Flow showed a significant increase in job satisfaction subsequent to the flow experience. It was also investigated how those high in job satisfaction experienced being in flow at work. Relative to those who were low in job satisfaction, those high in job satisfaction perceived the flow situation to be pleasant and joyful. In many of Csikszentmihalyi's interview studies, people have described the flow experience as intensely pleasurable (e.g., Csikszentmihalyi 2003; Csikszentmihalyi, 1997; Csikszentmihalyi, 1996). The analysis in the second article however showed a moderate correlation between job satisfaction and the pleasant / joyful-variables of the flow simplex structure. This means that the flow situation presently investigated was not as intense as the flow experiences Csikszentmihalyi refers to. Yet, most interviews conducted by Csikszentmihalyi are conducted in sports, leisure, or on top class business leaders (e.g., Csikszentmihalyi, 1996; Csikszentmihalyi & Csikszentmihalyi, 1992). Perhaps those situations provide flow experiences that are more intense and closer to peak experiences than the kind of flow tested in regular work settings. The sample of the present thesis is assumed to represent a diversified group whose responses presumably are typical of average urban Norwegian workers. Hence, these results imply that most people who experience flow in regular, ordinary work situations perceive such incidents as satisfying and pleased.

4.5 Practical implications

Psychometric implications regarding the flow construct arise due to the core characteristics of the flow state. Flow is a mental state engaged without conscious participation by the actor, which means that the experience can only be described and measured retrospectively. Even though research have managed to conceptualize the word flow through studies, it nevertheless remains difficult to measure (Jackson & Marsh, 1996; Kowal & Fortier, 1999; Mitchell, 1992).

Further implications arise due to the theoretical foundation of the thesis. The unified theory of flow presented in the introduction focuses extensively on the subconscious processes of behavior, which is particularly difficult to test empirically. In fact, the comparison and contrast analysis is far more comprehensive than what is empirically testable through the specifications of hypotheses and statistical analyses. Moreover, the extensive focus on subconscious processes complicates the use of self-completing questionnaires. Yet, few, if any, empirical research studies have been conducted on goal setting, flow, and work related variables. It was therefore necessary to establish a theoretical foundation prior to generating hypotheses. It is also a shortcoming of the present study that the data on which the thesis is based has not trained employees on a flow-program in advance. Thus we cannot conclude that the motivational effects of flow will last, as these results are based on the flow experiences *per se*. Further research should try to gather data after flow initiatives have been brought into effect.

Given these implications, it follows that the flow theory is quite demanding. Yet, flow involves several central aspects of the subconscious processes that characterize the working mind. This leaves us with no other option than to include our knowledge on flow when attempting to understand work behavior. The fact that most theories in organizational psychology have excluded the function of subconscious processes in research is yet another reason for including the flow theory in future studies. Hopefully, the present master thesis has managed to show why the flow theory deserves attention and how it may be an important contributor to organizational psychology.

4.6 Conclusion: Applicability of results

A major challenge faced by contemporary psychology is the implementation of research results into daily practice. Although several management programs are being developed within the branch of organizational psychology, most of our research results are never or rarely tested in real life. A crucial aspect of the flow theory developed in the present master thesis is the practical applicability of the results. To what extent can we actually make use of this knowledge? The main aim of this thesis was to theoretically and empirically test the possible relation between flow and work situations, yet a few careful suggestions will be made.

An organizational initiative would necessarily consist of two parts, namely a theoretical and a practical session. A theoretical introduction is important in order to make sure that employees manage to recognize the flow characteristics, and further relate these to his or her personal experiences. For this purpose, Csikszentmihalyi's flow theory makes a perfect contribution. Extensive use of examples, pictures, and open dialogues where employees are free to tell their stories will increase the likelihood of getting at grips with the flow state. The practical approach should aim at helping each employee to identify their present situation, to learn which of their work tasks that already induces flow experiences. One way of doing this is to write down the most important work tasks that constitute a normal work week. By inspection, employees should be able to appraise which of the tasks that provides interesting, joyful, and challenging experiences. The flow simplex may be used as a tool to evaluate their work tasks. All the seven bipolar adjectives of the flow simplex structure are relevant to interpreting subjective affective experiences towards personal work tasks. When these experiences are put on paper, they may be easier to recognize and consequently it is easier to identify the prerequisites of the flow state. This process will increase the self-awareness of subjective flow experiences, which presumably may help the employees to understand how to enhance their potentials.

When employees have mapped their work tasks and managed to relate their flow experience to these tasks, specific goal setting may facilitate flow experiences. The relation between goal setting and flow was only moderately supported in empirical analyses. Yet, previous research has proven goal setting to be a strong predictor of increased work performance (Arnold et al., 1998; Locke & Latham, 2002). The theoretical evaluation of the complementary features of goal setting and flow suggested that flow could explain many of the subconscious processes directed by goal setting behavior. It could be interesting to use goal setting as a technique, and test the effects it would have on flow.

Although not tested in the present master thesis, there are several other possible factors that could facilitate flow experiences at work. Team-work, specific characteristics of work tasks, personality traits, individual skills, and health issues are just a few variables that are likely to influence the flow experience. It remains to be investigated which of these variables that are most important. Nevertheless, in order to use flow as a resource, the bottom line is to approach work tasks in a manner that invites to flow. One suggestion is that this can be done through systematic goal setting. Most likely, the effects of this would be increased work performance, work motivation, and job satisfaction.

References

Abi-Hasem, N. (2000). Psychology, time, and culture [comment]. *American Psychologist, 55*(3), 342-343.

Arnold, J., Cooper, C. L. & Robertson, I. T. (1998). *Work psychology: Understanding human behaviour in the workplace*. Pearson Education Limited: Prentice Hall.

Audia, G., Kristof-Brown, A., Brown, K. G., & Locke, E.A., (1996). Relationship of goals and microlevel work processes to performance on a multipath manual task. *Journal of Applied Psychology 81*(5), 483-497.

Baumeister, R., Bratslavsky, E., & Finkenauer, C. (2001). Bad is stronger than good. *Review of General Psychology, 5*, 323-370.

Cameron, J., Banko, K. M., & Pierce, W. D. (2001). Pervasive negative effects of rewards on intrinsic motivation: The myth continues. *The Behavior Analyst, 24*, 1-44.

Csikszentmihalyi, M. (1975a). *Beyond boredom and anxiety*. San Francisco: Jossey-Bass.

Csikszentmihalyi, M. (1996). *Creativity: Flow and the psychology of discovery and invention*. New York: Harper Collins.

Csikszentmihalyi, M. (1997). *Finding flow. The psychology of engagement with everyday life*. New York: Basic Books.

Csikszentmihalyi, M. (2003). *Good business. Leadership, flow and the making of meaning*. London: Hodder and Stoughton.

Csikszentmihalyi, M. & Csikszentmihalyi, I. S. (1992). *Optimal experience: Psychological studies of flow in consciousness* (pp. 15-36). New York: Cambridge University Press.

Csikszentmihalyi, M. & LeFevre, J. (1989). Optimal experience in work and leisure. *Journal of Personality and Social Psychology 56*(5), 815-822.

Csikszentmihalyi, M. & Nakamura, J. (1999). Emerging goals and the self-regulation of behaviour. In RS Wyer jr (Ed). *Perspectives on behavioural self regulation* (pp. 107-118). Mahwah: N.J. Lawrence Erlbaum.

Eckblad, G. (1980). The curvex: Simple order structure revealed in ratings of complexity, interestingness, and pleasantness. *Scandinavian Journal of Psychology, 21*, 1-16.

Eckblad, G. (1981). *Schema theory: A conceptual framework of cognitive-motivational processes*. London: Academy Press.

Festinger, L. (1954). A theory of social comparison processes. *Human Relations, 7*, 117-140.

Gustafsson, J. E. & Stahl, P. A. (2000). *STREAMS user's guide. Version 2.5 for Windows*. Mölndal, Sweden: Mulitvariate Ware.

Guttman, L. (1954). A new approach to factor analysis: The radex. In P. F. Lazarsfeld (Ed.), *Mathematical thinking in the social sciences*. Glencoe: The Free Press. (Reissued New York: Russell & Russell, 1969).

Hackman, J. R. and Oldman, G. R. (1975). General job satisfactioin scale. In: Cook, J. D., Hepworthe, S. J., Wall, T. D. & Warr, P. B. (1981). *The experience of work: A compendium and review of 249 measures and their use*. London: Academic Press.

Han, S. (1992). The relationship between life satisfaction and flow in elderly korean immigrants. In M. Csikszentmihalyi & I. S. Csikszentmihalyi (Eds.). *Optimal experience: Psychological studies of flow in consciousness* (pp. 138-149). New York: Cambridge University Press.

Hills, P., Argyle, M., & Reeves, R. (2000). Individual differences in leisure satisfactions: An investigation of four theories of leisure motivation. *Personality and Individual Differences 28*, 763-779.

Jackson, S. A. & Marsh, H. W. (1996). Development and validation of a scale to measure optimal experience: The flow state scale. *Journal of Sport and Exercise Psychology, 18*, 17-35.

Jackson, S. A., Thomas, P. R., Marsh, H. W., & Smethurst, C. J. (2001). Relationships between flow, self-concept, psychological skills, and performance. *Journal of Applied Sport Pscyhology, 13*, 129-153.

Jørskog, K. G. & Sörbom, D. (1993). *LISREL 8. Structural equation modelling with SIMPLIS command language*. Hillsdale NJ: Erlbaum.

Kahneman, D. (1999). Objective happiness. In D. Kahneman, E. Diener, & N. Schwarz (Eds.), *Well-being: The foundations of hedonic psychology* (pp. 3-25). New York: Russell Sage Foundation.

Kanfer, R. & Ackerman, P. L. (1989). Motivation and cognitive abilities: An integrative/aptitude-treatment interaction approach to skill acquisition. *Journal of Applied Psychology, 74*(4), 657-690.

Kowal, J. & Fortier, M. S. (1999). Motivational determinants of flow: Contributions from self-determination theory. *The Journal of Social Psychology 139*(3), 355-368.

Larson, R. (1992). Flow in Writing. In M. Csikszentmihalyi & I. S. Csikszentmihalyi (Eds.). *Optimal experience: Psychological studies of flow in consciousness* (pp. 172-182). New York: Cambridge University Press.

Lawler, E. E. & Hall, D. T. (1970). Internal work motivation scale. In Cook, J. D., Hepworthe, S. J., Wall, T. D. & Warr, P. B. (1981). *The experience of work: A compendium and review of 249 measures and their use.* London: Academic Press.

LeFevre, J. (1992). Flow and the quality of experiences during work and leisure. In M. Csikszentmihalyi & I. S. Csikszentmihalyi (Eds.). *Optimal experience: Psychological studies of flow in consciousness* (pp. 307-319). New York: Cambridge University Press.

Locke, E. A. (1997). The motivation to work: What we know. In M. Maehr & P. Pintrich (Eds.), *Advances in Motivation and Achievement (10),* 375-412. Greenwich, CT: JAI Press.

Locke, E. A. & Latham, G. P. (2002). Building a practically useful theory of goal setting and task motivation. *American Psychologist 59(9)*, 705-717.

Locke, E. A. & Latham, G. P. (1990). *A theory of goal setting and task performance.* USA: Prentice Hall.

Mabe, P. A., & West, S. G. (1982). Validity of self-evaluation of ability: A review and meta-analysis. *Journal of Applied Psychology, 67*, 280-296.

Marr, A. J. (2001). In the Zone: A biobehavioral theory of the flow experience. *The Online Journal of Sport Psychology 31,* 1-7. Benecom Technologies Inc.

Massimini, F., Csikszentmihalyi, M. & Delle Fave, A. (1992). Flow and biocultural evolution. In M. Csikszentmihalyi & I. S. Csikszentmihalyi (Eds.). *Optimal experience: Psychological studies of flow in consciousness* (pp. 60-85). New York: Cambridge University Press.

Mitchell, R. G. jr. (1992). Sociological implications of the flow experience. In M. Csikszentmihalyi & I. S. Csikszentmihalyi (Eds.). *Optimal experience: Psychological studies of flow in consciousness* (pp. 36-60). New York: Cambridge University Press.

Porter, L. W., & Lawler, E. E. (1968). *Managerial attitudes and performance.* Homewood, IL: Irwin-Dorsey.

Singer, J. A., & Salovey, P. (1993). The remembered self: Emotion and memory in personality. New York: The Free Press.

Straume, L. V. (2004a). *Flow in organizational psychology: A psychometric approach to the relations between goal setting, flow, and work motivation.* 1st Article of Master Thesis in Psychology, NTNU. Unpublished material.

Thomas, D. L. & Diener, E. (1990). Memory accuracy in the recall of emotions. *Journal of Personality and Social Pscyhology, 59*(2), 291-297.

Vitterso, J. (1998). *Happy people and wonderful experiences: Structure and predictors of subjective well-being*. Doctoral dissertation, University of Tromsø.

Vitterso, J. (2004). Subjective well-being versus self-actualization: Using the flow-simplex to promote a conceptual clarification of subjective quality of life. *Social Indicators Research, 65*, 299-331.s

Vitterso, J. & Kjøndahl, C. (2003). Measuring flow: Comparing three scales. Paper presented at *The 5th Conference of the International Society of Quality-of-Life Studies*, Frankfurt, Germany July 20-24.

Vitterso, J., Vorkinn, M., & Vistad, O. I. (2001). Congruence between recreational mode and actual behavior – a prerequisite for optimal experience. *Journal of Leisure Research, 33*(2), 137-159.

Wicklund, R. A. (1986). Orientation to the environment versus preoccupation with human potential. In R. M. Sorrentino & E. T. Higgins (Eds.), *Handbook of motivation and cognition. Foundations of social behaviour* (Vol 1, pp. 64-95). London: Guilford Press.

Flow in Organizational Psychology:

A Psychometric Approach to Relations between Goal-setting, Flow, and Work Motivation

1st Article of Master Thesis in Psychology
Lisa Vivoll Straume

Department of Psychology, Norwegian University of Science and Technology
Trondheim, Norway
Spring 2004

Abstract

The core aim of the present article was to test the psychometric quality of Jackson & Marsh's (1996) Flow State Scale (FSS), and the associations between goal setting, flow, and work motivation. Prior to the data collection process, some of the FSS items were rewritten in order to make the scale apt to measure flow in work settings. Consequently, dimensionality, reliability, internal consistency, and discriminant validity of the revised version had to be tested. The sample consisted of 170 employees from 9 different organizations in the middle part of Norway, representing occupations from technology, financial departments, medical business, social services, and salesmen. Results indicated that an eight-dimensional structure of flow may suit work settings better than the original nine-dimensional structure, although the differences were small. Furthermore, only two of the flow dimensions were significantly related both to work motivation and goal setting, i.e. the clear goal dimension and the autotelic dimension. The same two flow dimensions were significantly related to goal setting, indicating that these two are the most important characteristics of flow in work settings. Based on the theoretical analysis given introductory and the results of the empirical analyses, it is suggested that goal setting may be a functional technique applicable to increase levels of flow in work settings. Furthermore, increased levels of flow may contribute to increased levels of work motivation.

1.0 Flow, work motivation and goal setting

Psychological flow is a positive experiential state of deep concentration and absorption. While in this state, people lose awareness of time, the surroundings, and the awareness of their own performance (Csikszentmihalyi, 1975; Kowal & Fortier, 1999). Flow tends to occur when a person's skills are fully involved in overcoming challenges. Furthermore, flow is intrinsically rewarding, thus functioning as positive reinforcement for the task at hand. A natural assumption would thus be that flow is an important resource suitable for organizational initiatives aimed at increasing work motivation. Accordingly, an aim of the present paper is to empirically test the relation between flow and work motivation.

In order to explore flow in relation to work issues such as job motivation, we need measurement procedures that allows for comparison among psychological constructs (Jackson & Marsh, 1996). Jackson and Marsh (1996) have developed and validated the Flow State Scale (FSS), a measurement questionnaire that assesses flow in sports and physical activity settings. Prior to the study presented in this article, the original version of the Flow State Scale was revised in order to fit data collection in work settings. The development of a psychometrically valid scale applicable to work settings may facilitate quantitatively based investigations of flow, which can be applied in psychological research. A major aim of this paper is to validate the revised version of the flow state scale in order to provide a measurement instrument that assesses flow as a multidimensional construct in organizational psychology.

It is of interest that research on flow in work settings has extended value, i.e. other than only detecting relations among psychological concepts. However, using the flow theory in organizational initiatives aimed at increasing work motivation require functional techniques for entering the flow state. The present article suggests that goal setting may function as an important technique for entering and sustaining the flow state in work activities. Consequently, the relation between goal setting and flow is tested.

1.1 The flow construct
The flow state has been described at length by Csikszentmihalyi (e.g., 1975, 1997, 2003), and further substantiated by others (Jackson & Marsh, 1996; Kowal & Fortier, 1999; LeFevre, 1992; Marr, 2001). However, due to the inherent difficulties of applying empirical methods to

phenomenological experiences, the research on flow has not been devoted the psychological investigation it deserves (Jackson & Marsh, 1996). Psychological flow is largely an inside-the-head experience and would require considerable detailed corroboration to satisfy scientific scrutiny. Thus, its characteristics make it difficult to be defined, observed, and tested. Flow simply lacks the concrete objectivity a pragmatic psychological concept calls for (Csikszentmihalyi & Csikszentmihalyi, 1992; Hills, Argyle, & Reeves, 2000). This implies that we lack the terms and expressions necessary in order to describe the phenomenon in a satisfactory manner. Nevertheless, a growing body of research articles has provided important knowledge that has made it possible to get at grips with what flow is and how it works.

Psychological flow consists of a variety of positive experiential characteristics. In attempting to conceptualize the flow experience, Csikszentmihalyi (1975a, 1997, 2003) and Jackson and Marsh (1996) have identified nine dimensions that describe and constitute the factors necessary to enter and sustain the flow state. The dimensions are (1) challenge-skill balance, meaning that the flow state involves a fine balance between the challenges of a task and one's ability to meet with those challenges; (2) action-awareness merging, because flow implies a total involvement of the activity; (3) loss of self-consciousness, as attention is exclusively focused on the task at hand; (4) clear goals, because they function as rules for action that make it possible for the person to perform without questioning what should be done; (5) unambiguous feedback, provided by the gut feeling one gets from doing the right things while working on a task; (6) sense of control, manifested through the feeling of doing the right things; (7) total concentration on task at hand; (8) transformation of time, in that it alters perceptibly; and (9) the experience is autotelic, i.e. it is intrinsically rewarding (for an elaborated description of the nine dimensions, see Jackson & Marsh, 1996). For the purpose of theoretical clarity, the present article suggests that these nine dimensions should be divided in three major categories. The challenge-skill and the clear goal dimension can be described as *prerequisite* characteristics of flow, as both constitute features that need to be present prior to entering the flow state. The next category is *immediate* characteristics of flow, capturing action-awareness merging, loss of self-consciousness, unambiguous feedback, sense of control, total concentration on the task at hand, and transformation of time. All these represent the core, ever-present feeling of being in flow. Finally, the third category is the *subsequent* characteristics of flow, namely the autotelic experience.

The construction and validation of the Flow State Scale (FSS) was based on the nine-dimensional structure of flow because they were assumed to be important characteristics of flow in sports activities. Thus, it is generally interesting to investigate if all these nine dimensions are equally important for the flow experience in work activities.

1.2 The flow state scale revised

Because the Flow State Scale (FSS) was developed to measure flow in sport and physical activity settings, it was not entirely suited to measure flow in work settings. It was particularly interesting to test the FSS on work activities since no quantitative research has been conducted on flow in organizational psychology. Prior to the data collection, some of the items of the FSS were modified. Furthermore, it was unclear whether the flow experience at work would include all nine dimensions present in other situational settings such as sports and physical activities. However, the richness and complexity of a construct such as flow necessitates measurements that are inclusive rather than exclusive (Jackson & Marsh, 1996). Thus, the original form of the questionnaire was kept, only making minor adjustments to fit the work situation. Further details on this process are given in the method section. Based on the changes described above, an important aim of this article is to test the reliability of the revised flow state scale.

1.3 Psychological flow and work motivation

Flow leaves the person feeling motivated to continue engaging in the given flow-activity (Csikszentmihalyi, 2003; Jackson & Marsh, 1996; Kowal & Fortier, 1999; Larson, 1992). Most of these findings however are accomplished in sport activities, leisure hobbies and educational settings, as the majority of the research has been conducted in these areas. In one of his recent books, Csikszentmihalyi (2003) does argue that flow is also motivating in work settings. This statement is based on the interviews of several business employees, especially executives in daily charge. However, he does not refer to any empirical analyses that report general tendencies of correspondences between flow and work motivation. Thus, it was necessary to investigate this phenomenon among several employees in different occupations.

Flow is related to motivation in two manners. Firstly, flow provides an instant motivation to fulfill the task at hand. Balance of challenges and skills, perceived control, and total involvement constitute an inspiration to continue. Secondly, flow function as positive reinforcement. According to general principles of learning psychology, this will motivate the person to seek the same tasks over again because he or she has learned what motivating effects the experience had (Marr, 2001). In both instances, behavior is driven by intrinsic motivation, i.e. without any reward other than that provided by the activity itself.

Motivational theories in psychology have a tradition of distinguishing between intrinsic and extrinsic motivation. Several studies show that adding external rewards reduce, and in some cases even eliminate, the initial internal motivation. If so be it, stimulating employees to work by means of internal motivation would be impossible because the work domain is mainly based on the principle of external rewards. Yet, Cameron, Banko and Pierce (2001) conducted a meta analysis on existing research results, which concluded that the empirical basis of the motivation theory was not sufficient to sustain the conclusion. The interactive effect of both types of motivation would probably serve to explain general work motivation in a better way. Porter and Lawler (1968) have argued that optimal work performance occurs when there is a combination of intrinsic motivating work tasks, and external rewards are added.

Kowal and Fortier (1999) discuss the ambiguous findings on the relation between internal and external motivation and psychological flow. On the one hand, Csikszentmihalyi and LeFevre (1989) found positive correlations between intrinsic motivation and flow. On the contrary, Mannell, Zuzanek and Larson (1988, in Kowal & Fortier, 1999) found that frequency of the flow experience increased with external motivating rewards. Still others have found that both types of motivation are related to flow (e. g. Hills et al., 2000).

An important aim of the present paper is to investigate whether flow experiences lead to increased levels of work motivation. Most research projects on flow and motivation have proven intrinsic motivation to be the primary motivational effect of flow. Accordingly, it is hypothesized that flow is positively related to intrinsic motivation.

1.4 Goal setting as a predictor of flow experiences

Goal setting theory explains primarily how systematic goal setting can influence the growth of positive work behavior such as efficacy. Most importantly, specific and difficult goals are found to be the most effective generator of high work performance, as opposed to general and easy goals (Arnold, Cooper & Robertson, 1998; Locke & Latham, 2002; Locke, 1997). According to Locke and Latham (2002), four different mechanisms influence how goals affect performance. First of all, goals direct *attention* and *effort* towards activities that are relevant for reaching the goal, i.e. help the person to focus on strategies that will most efficiently lead him or her towards the completion of a task. Second, goals have an *energizing* function in that high goals lead to greater effort than do low goals. Third, goals affect *endurance* in that high goals prolong effort when participants are allowed to control the time they spend on a task. Fourth, there is an indirect affection of *action* in that goals lead to arousal, discovery and use of task-relevant knowledge and strategies (Locke & Latham, 2002).

An interesting inquiry about goal setting theory is the reason *why* goals prove to affect performance in such manners as given above. To understand this inquiry, it may help to focus on the mental processes through which the goal-reaching motivation is sustained. Consider the four mechanisms given above, i.e. affecting attention, energy, endurance and discovery of task-relevant knowledge. It is suggested that these mechanisms affect performance because they represent components that enable people to enter and sustain the flow state. Firstly, goals direct attention which is one of the most important elements of flow. Goals force the attention to be focused on a limited area of stimuli, enabling the person to grow into a deep concentration resembling that of flow. Second, it could be argued that the energizing function of goals only is present as long as the flow state is operative. If an external factor distracts the attention away from the goal reaching action, they no longer have an energizing function, at least not until attention again is focused on reaching the goal. The third mechanism stated that goals affect endurance in that high goals prolong effort. Now, why is endurance a consequence of goal setting? Goal setting enables the person to invest his psychic energy in a limited set of behavioral strategies, namely those that will lead to reaching the set goal. Several informants in flow research have explained that the flow state increases the endurance of behavior because they were able to concentrate their psychic energy in the task at hand (Massimini, Delle Fave, & Csikszentmihalyi, 1992; Nakamura, 1992).

The fourth mechanism described by Locke and Latham (2002) states that goals has an indirect affect on action in that they lead to arousal, discovery and use of task-relevant knowledge and strategies. The theory does not explain the mental processes through which this is possible. However, if a person can discover and use task-relevant knowledge and strategies, it implies that this knowledge already exists in the mind but is not available to consciousness until the knowledge is activated by the goals. Eckblad (1981) uses scheme theory to describe the optimal experience of flow, an approach that may serve to further explain the goal affect. According to Eckblad (1981), schemes are assumed to be responsible for the normal functioning of an individual. Schemes are seen as organized sequences of mental operations, functioning within a hierarchic system. This hierarchic system consists of smaller units of schemes continuously operative, and the particular scheme active will depend on the situation we encounter. Specifying the goals for action in advance will limit the potential schemes that can be activated. Hence, the person is more likely to make use of task-relevant strategies because the possible schemes that potentially can be activated are limited. Shortly stated, the schemes associated with irrelevant task strategies are ruled out. This leads to the suggestion that goals indirectly affect the discovery of task-relevant strategies because it activates the schemes relevant to reach the set goal.

What distinguishes psychological flow from goal setting theory is the treatment of and the focus on consciousness. Flow focuses primarily on the mental processes occurring subconsciously when a person is absorbed in solving a task. Goal setting theory in general focuses primarily on how goals are consciously defined in advance of the goal reaching actions. It further elaborates on mediating and moderating effects such as attention, effort, persistence, as well as feedback, commitment and monetary incentives, respectively. A contribution to goal setting theory would be to explain the subconscious processes that is operative during the goal setting and goal reaching actions.

As shown in the description above, goal setting actions have certain affects on performance that resemble those described in the flow theory. A natural assumption for scientific scrutiny would be the following: Goal setting actions may increase the occurrence of flow, provided that the rules for productive goal setting are followed. Accordingly, it is hypothesized that individuals high on personal goal setting will experience more flow.

1.5 Aims of the study
A short sum up of the specific research question presented in the previous sections will clarify the main aims of the present article.
   4. In an attempt to make the FSS apt to measure flow in work setting, some of the items were rewritten prior to the data collection process. Consequently, dimensionality, reliability, internal consistency, and discriminant validity of the revised version need

to be tested. Furthermore, it is interesting to investigate whether all nine dimensions of the FSS are equally important to work settings as they are to sports activities.

5. Based on previous findings in sport and physical activity studies, research has shown that flow increases motivation. Accordingly, it is hypothesized that flow increases employees' experience of work motivation. Because flow is experienced as satisfactory, satisfaction is assumed to function as a complementary predictor of work motivation.

6. Based on the theoretical evaluation of goal setting and flow given above, the third aim of the paper is to investigate the effects of goal setting on flow. It is assumed that the act of goal setting will contribute to increased levels of the flow experience.

2.0 Method

2.1 Sample

Data was collected through a self-completing questionnaire survey. The sample consists of 170 employees at 9 different organizations in Norway, representing occupations from technology, financial departments, medical business, social services, and salesmen. Initially, 12 different organizations were invited to participate in the present study, all of whom were selected from the list of customers in a consulting company in Trondheim. The executives in daily charge of each workplace were invited to include their employees in the study. Nine of these gave their approval for the distribution of questionnaires to the potential respondents, i.e. the employees. All the attendants were informed in advance that the data would be treated confidentially. Of the 400 questionnaires distributed, 170 were returned, which gives a response rate of 42,5 %.

Of the 170 participants, 78 were women and 91 were men. One participant did not specify gender. Average age of the group was 38 years (SD = 9.0), 54 % had university education, 96 % worked full time.

2.2 Questionnaires

Flow State Scale. A scale developed by Jackson and Marsh (1996) was used to measure level and intensity of the flow experience at work. The Flow State Scale (FSS) consists of 36 items and is based on a nine-dimensional structure of flow. Flow was assessed on a 5-point Likert-type scale ranging from strongly disagree to strongly agree.

The questionnaire was initially translated into Norwegian by three individual translators, and then translated back to English by different persons in order to discover potential discrepancies. Some of the items were revised in order to suit a work situation instead of a sport situation. The original form of the questionnaire was kept, making only minor adjustments to fit the work situation. The final version was worked out in a discussion group using all available suggestions. Before responding to the flow state scale, respondents were asked to recall a specific situation at work where they experienced being totally absorbed in a task. In order to keep in mind the flow experience while responding to the items, they were asked to write down the particular situation in mind.

Work motivation. A scale developed and validated by Lawler and Hall (1970) was used to assess work motivation. The scale consists of four items graded on a 5-point Likert-type scale ranging from strongly disagree to strongly agree.

Job satisfaction. A three-item scale developed and validated by Hackman and Oldman (1975) assessed job satisfaction. The items were graded on a 5-point Likert-type scale ranging from strongly disagree to strongly agree.

Goal setting. A two-dimensional scale consisting of nine items was used to measure personal goal setting and organizational goals. All the items were based on a systematic theoretical inquiry of Locke and Latham's (1990) goal setting theory, most of which were selected from their own questionnaire. The original questionnaire by Locke and Latham consisted of 54 items, which was too comprehensive to include in the present study.

2.3 Statistical analyses

Principal Component Analysis with iteration and varimax rotation was applied on all measurement questionnaires to detect the underlying dimensions of the items. Structural Equation Modelling Made Simple (STREAMS) offers a consistent interface to the LISREL program and was used for confirmatory factor analysis of flow (Gustafsson & Stahl, 2000; Jørskog & Sørbom, 1993). Chronbach's alpha coefficient evaluated the internal consistency of the indices. Average total inter item correlations were also calculated, and correlation coefficients were used to measure discriminant validity. Stepwise regression analyses and hierarchical block regressions were carried out to test the relationship between flow, work motivation and goal setting.

3.0 Results

3.1 Dimensional structure and reliability the Flow State Scale.

Exploratory analysis of dimensionality using Principal Component Analysis was first carried out to see whether the nine dimensions found by Jackson and Marsh (1996) could be replicated. The structure revealed by the present analysis deviated from the original in that it suggested ten instead of nine dimensions. Two of these ten factors contained only one variable, item 1 which originally belonged to the challenge-skill dimension and item 35 which originally belonged to the time-alteration dimension. Item 19 loaded both on the challenge-skill dimension where it originally belonged, and the clear goal dimension, which means that it was uncertain what the item actually measured. Two variables from the clear goal dimension (v 3 and v 12), one variable from the feedback-control dimension (v 33), and one variable from the concentration dimension (v 14) all loaded quite low in the dimensional structure suggested. Furthermore, all four variables from both the original feedback dimension and control dimension clustered together as one factor, which means that the analysis did not distinguish between the two types of flow characteristics. The explorative model of the flow state scale explained 69 % of the variance in flow. For details concerning the items, see Appendix B.

A new Principal Component Analysis was run, this time asking for nine dimensions, still attempting to replicate Jackson and Marsh's (1996) nine-dimensional flow structure. The factor loadings from this analysis still did not equal the one suggested by Jackson and Marsh (1996). Item 1, 3, 12, 14, 19, 33 and 35 did not load clear enough to indicate a good fit to a nine-dimensional model. These were the same items with ambiguous factor loadings in the first analysis, with factor loadings varying from .30 to .45 on more than one dimension. Items from the feedback and the control dimension did still cluster together as one dimension.

Due to the results given above, a new exploratory analysis was further specified, this time excluding the variables with ambiguous factor loadings, i.e. variable 1, 3, 12, 14, 19, 33 and 35. The structure now revealed eight dimensions, with factor loadings indicating a better fit to the data than the original model given by Jackson and Marsh (1996). Both the challenge-skill dimension and the clear goal dimension now consisted of two instead of four variables. Three variables loaded on the concentration dimension and three on the time alteration dimension. The feedback and the control dimension were still clustering together, indicating that these two factors cannot be distinguished. Overall, the new eight-dimensional model of the flow state scale explained 68,3 % of the variance in flow. Comparisons of the factor loadings of the nine-dimensional and the eight-dimensional flow state scales are given in table 1 (Factor loadings for the flow state scale variables).

The new eight-dimensional flow state scale demonstrated a slightly stronger internal consistency and reliability than the nine-dimensional structure suggested by Jackson and Marsh (1996). Only the concentration dimension had a stronger alpha in the nine-dimensional structure, all other dimensions demonstrated stronger reliability in the eight-dimensional structure. According to Nunnally (1978) Chronbach's alpha should ideally be above .70. Inter item correlation should be above .30. Comparisons of the Chronbach's alphas and inter item correlations of the nine-dimensional and the eight-dimensional flow state scales are given in table 3 (Reliability Flow State Scale).

To compare the fit of the factor models found in the exploratory analysis, confirmatory factor analyses were further specified using STREAMS/LISREL. The analysis of the nine-factor model revealed an RMSEA of .058. An RMSEA of .070 or lower is generally considered as a proper indicator of fit to an original model, yet the lower the better. The eight-factor model gained an RMSEA of .049 after allowing two of the items in the feedback/control dimension to load on the self-consciousness dimension. These results indicate that the eight-factor structure demonstrates a better fit to the data than the original model. Factor loadings with item specifications for the eight-dimensional flow state scale are given in table 2 (Factor loadings for variables of the eight-dimensional Flow State Scale).

Discriminant validity. By investigating the correlations between the dimensions it is possible to determine discriminant validity of the structures. Although factor analyses showed that flow can be divided in eight instead of nine dimensions, discriminant validity may further explain whether the dimensions actually measure different aspects of the same phenomenon. Accordingly, dimensions should correlate at a moderate level. Too high correlations would indicate that the dimensions cannot be distinguished. Correlation coefficients of the nine dimensional model showed that there was a strong association between the feedback and control dimension ($r = .64$). Thus, it could be argued that including these two dimensions as one would be a better option than to keep them distinct. The results indicate that the eight-dimensional model seems to find slightly better support through statistical procedures. All correlations are presented in table 4 and 5 (Inter-correlations among dimensions).

Table 1
Factor loadings for the flow state scale variables

Dimension original model	Variable item FSS	Factor loadings Original model	Dimension new model	Variable item FSS	Factor loadings New model
Single new factor	v 1	.52			--
F1 Challenge /skill	v 10	.84	F1 Challenge / skill	v 10	.82
F1 Challenge / skill	v 19	.48			--
F1 Challenge / skill	v 28	.83	F1 Challenge / skill	v 28	.88
F2 Merging self / act.	v 2	.67	F2 Merging self / act.	v 2	.68
F2 Merging self / act.	v 11	.74	F2 Merging self / act.	v 11	.73
F2 Merging self / act.	v 20	.74	F2 Merging self / act.	v 20	.76
F2 Merging self / act.	v 29	.76	F2 Merging self / act.	v 29	.77
F3 Clear goals	v 3	.52			--
F3 Clear goals	v 30	.77	F3 Clear goals	v 30	.83
F3 Clear goals	v 21	.76	F3 Clear goals	v 21	.81
F4 Feedback / control	v 12	.46	F3 Clear goals		--
F4 Feedback / control	v 4	.63	F4 Feedback / control	v 4	.67
F4 Feedback / control	v 13	.74	F4 Feedback / control	v 13	.80
F4 Feedback / control	v 22	.63	F4 Feedback / control	v 22	.68
F4 Feedback / control	v 31	.61	F4 Feedback / control	v 31	.62
F4 Feedback / control	v 6	.65	F4 Feedback / control	v 6	.69
F4 Feedback / control	v 15	.59	F4 Feedback / control	v 15	.56
F4 Feedback / control	v 24	.66	F4 Feedback / control	v 24	.66
F4 Feedback / control	v 33	.50			--
F5 Concentration	v 5	.71	F5 Concentration	v 5	.73
F5 Concentration	v 14	.43			--
F5 Concentration	v 23	.64	F5 Concentration	v 23	.67
F5 Concentration	v 32	.78	F5 Concentration	v 32	.81
F6 Loss of self-cons.	v 7	.78	F6 Loss of self-cons.	v 7	.78
F6 Loss of self-cons.	v 16	.76	F6 Loss of self-cons.	v 16	.77
F6 Loss of self-cons.	v 25	.76	F6 Loss of self-cons.	v 25	.74
F6 Loss of self-cons.	v 34	.85	F6 Loss of self-cons.	v 34	.85
F7 Time alteration	v 8	.78	F7 Time alteration	v 8	.81
F7 Time alteration	v 17	.77	F7 Time alteration	v 17	.77
F7 Time alteration	v 26	.73	F7 Time alteration	v 26	.72
F7 Time alteration	v 35	.40	F7 Time alteration		--
F9 Autotelic exp.	v 9	.69	F8 Autotelic exp.	v 9	.72
F9 Autotelic exp.	v 18	.72	F8 Autotelic exp.	v 18	.72
F9 Autotelic exp.	v 27	.79	F8 Autotelic exp.	v 27	.82
F9 Autotelic exp.	v 36	.80	F8 Autotelic exp.	v 36	.81

Note: N = 164-170. Variable item no. 1, 3, 12, 14, 19, 33 and 35 were removed prior to the analysis presented of the new model in the table.

Table 2 Factor loadings for variables of the eight-dimensional Flow State Scale

Dimensions and variables	Factor loadings							
	1	2	3	4	5	6	7	8
Feedback / Control								
13. I was aware of how well I was performing.	.79							
6. I felt in total control of what I was doing.	.72							
22. While working on this task, I had a good idea about how well I was doing.	.59							
4. It was really clear to me that I was doing well.	.70							
24. I had a feeling of total control.	.64	.20						
31. I could tell by the way I was performing how well I was doing.	.72	-.24						
15. I felt like I could control what I was doing.	.55							
Loss of self-consciousness								
34. I was not worried about what others may have been thinking of me.		.87						
7. I was not concerned with what others may have been thinking of me.		.73						
16. I was not worried about my performance during the task.		.81						
25. I was not concerned with how I was presenting myself.		.62						
Autotelic experience								
27. The experience left me feeling good.			.80					
36. I found the experience extremely rewarding.			.76					
18. I loved the feeling of that performance and want to capture it again.			.72					
9. I really enjoyed the experience.			.78					
Merging of self and action								
29. I did things spontaneously and automatically without having to think.				.70				
20. I performed automatically.				.64				
11. Things just seemed to happen automatically.				.75				
2. I took the right decisions without thinking about trying to do so.				.66				
Time alteration								
8. Time seemed to alter (either slowed down or speeded up).					.76			
17. The way time passed seemed to be different from normal.					.87			
26. It felt like time stopped while I was working on this task.					.53			
Concentration on task at hand								
32. I was completely focused on the task at hand.						.75		
5. My attention was focused entirely on what I was doing.						.59		
23. I had total concentration.						.63		
Clear goals								
30. My goals were clearly defined.							.83	
21. I knew what I wanted to achieve.							.79	
Challenge / skill balance								
28. The challenge and my skills were at an equally high level.								.72
10. My knowledge matched the high challenge of the task.								.94

Note: N = 164-170; Item 1, 3, 12, 14, 19, 33, and 35 excluded from original model 36-item model; Root Mean Square Approximation (RMSEA) = 0.049, Non-Normed Fit Index (NNFI) = 0.95, Comparative Fit Index (CFI) = 0.95

Table 3
Reliability Flow State Scale

Dimension FSS	Original Model FSS		Dimension FSS	Exploratory Model FSS	
	alpha	Average total inter item correlation		alpha	Average total inter item correlation
1. Challenge/skill v 1, 10, 19, 28	.739	.54	1. Challenge/skill v 10, 28	**.818**	.70
2. Merging v 2, 11, 20, 29	.783	.59	2. Merging v 2, 11, 20, 29	.783	.59
3. Clear goals v 3, 12, 21, 30	.773	.58	3. Clear goals v 21, 30	**.782**	.64
4. Feedback v 4, 13, 22, 31	.788	.60	4. Feedb./Control v 4, 6, 13, 15, 22, 24, 31	**.849**	.61
5. Control v 6, 15, 24, 33	.770	.58			
6. Concentration v 5, 14, 23, 32	.721	.52	5. Concentration v 5, 23, 32	**.693**	.52
7. Loss of self-cons v 7, 16, 25, 34	.837	.67	6. Loss of self-cons v 7, 16, 25, 34	.837	.67
8. Time v 8, 17, 26, 35	.737	.53	7. Time v 8, 17, 26	**.760**	.59
9. Autotelic v 9, 18, 27, 36	.846	.69	8. Autotelic v 9, 18, 27, 36	.846	.69

Note. N = 164-170; v = variables included in each dimension.

Table 4
Inter-correlations among dimensions in nine-factor structure

Dimension	1	2	3	4	5	6	7	8
1 Challenge/skill								
2 Merging	,17*							
3 Clear goals	,53**	,12						
4 Feedback	,46**	,19*	,54**					
5 Concentration	,37**	,09	,49**	,36**				
6 Control	,47**	,30**	,48**	,64**	,36**			
7 Loss of self-cons.	,19*	,41**	,18*	,16*	,17*	,41**		
8 Time alteration	,13	,31**	,14	,33**	,16*	,29**	,18*	
9 Autotelic exp.	,45**	,26**	,37**	,45**	,36**	,40**	,21**	,43**

Note. N=164-170. ** = p< .01; * = p< .05 (2-tailed).

Table 5
Inter-correlations among dimensions in eight-factor structure

Dimension	1	2	3	4	5	6	7
1 Challenge/skill							
2 Merging	,16*						
3 Clear goals	,27**	,02					
4 Feedback/control	,42**	,27**	,39**				
5 Concentration	,27**	,08	,37**	,36**			
6 Loss of self-cons.	,15	,41**	,13	,31**	,14		
7 Time alteration	,18*	,26**	,19*	,30**	,16*	,16*	
8 Autotelic exp.	,33	,26**	,31**	,46**	,33**	,21**	,44*

Note. N=164-170. ** = p< .01; * = p< .05 (2-tailed).

3.2 Dimensional structure and reliability of motivation and satisfaction

Exploratory factor analysis using Principal Component Analysis was executed on both the motivation scale and the satisfaction scale in order to appraise dimensionality structure of the variables. All four items in Lawler and Halls (1970) motivation scale clustered together in one dimension (factor loadings from .77 to .85). Reliability analysis demonstrated an alpha of .81. All three items from Hackman and Oldmans (1975) general job satisfaction scale did also cluster together as one dimension with factor loadings varying from .76 to .89. Chronbach's alpha on this scale was .76.

3.3 Factors related to work motivation

Mean, standard deviation and percentage experienced motivation and flow is presented in table 6a and b. One-way analysis of variance (ANOVA) was first carried out to see if differences in work motivation were due to demographic variables. None of the independent variables, i.e. age, gender, marital status, type of education and years of education were significantly related to work motivation.

Predictors of work motivation based on the nine-dimensional structure. Stepwise multiple regression analysis was executed to see if there was a significant correspondence between flow and work motivation. The nine dimensions of flow suggested by Jackson and Marsh (1996) were entered as the independent variables. The analysis showed that only two of the flow dimensions made a significant contribution, i.e. the autotelic and the clear goal dimension (beta = .34 $p < .001$; beta = .24 $p < .001$, respectively). Altogether, these two flow dimensions explained 23 % of the variance in work motivation (Adjusted R^2 = .23 $p < .001$).

Table 6a
Percentage of experienced motivation

	Very High	High	Medium	Low	M	SD
Work motivation	18 %	70 %	11 %	1 %	4,3	.48

Note. N = 164-170

Table 6b
Percentage of experienced flow – New Model, 8 Dimensions

Dimension of FSS	Very High	High	Medium	Low	M	SD
1. Challenge / skill	13 %	60 %	20 %	7 %	4,0	.70
2. Merging self / act.	6 %	18 %	36 %	44 %	3.0	.84
3. Clear goals	26 %	52 %	19 %	2 %	4,1	.69
4. Feedback / control	6 %	45 %	48 %	6 %	3,8	.54
5. Concentration	12 %	65 %	21 %	1 %	4,1	.56
6. Loss of self-cons	3 %	38 %	36 %	23 %	3,5	.85
7. Time alteration	3 %	23 %	52 %	23 %	3,3	.77
8. Autotelic	13 %	55 %	28 %	4 %	4,1	.61

Note. N = 164-170

Hierarchical block regression analysis was then executed to test the significance of the contributions of additional independent variables. It was hypothesized that flow and job satisfaction were important predictors of work motivation, with flow being the main contributor. Consequently, the two flow dimensions autotelic experience and clear goals were entered as the first and the second block, respectively. Furthermore, job satisfaction was entered as the third block. Only one variable was included in each block as the primary interest was to determine if the raise in explained variance was significant (F-change). All together, the independent variables explained 25 % of the variance in work motivation (Adjusted R^2 = .25 p < .001). The results are presented in table 7 as a comparison of the same analysis executed on the eight-dimensional flow structure.

Predictors of work motivation based on the eight-dimensional structure. A new stepwise multiple regression analysis was executed, now entering the *eight* dimensions of flow as the independent variables. The analysis still showed that only the autotelic and the clear goal dimension made a significant contribution, yet this analysis gave a slightly stronger beta coefficient (Autotelic experience: beta = .35 p < .001; Clear goals: beta = .28 p < .001). Altogether, these two flow dimensions explained 25 % of the variance in work motivation (Adjusted R^2 = .25 p < .001), indicating that the eight-dimensional flow structure is more sensitive to work motivation.

Hierarchal block regression analysis was executed using the same variables as the above block regression analysis. However, this time the two flow dimensions autotelic experience and clear goals were computed based on the eight-dimensional factor structure. When including all dimensions in a hierarchical block regression, the independent variables explained 27 % of the variance in work motivation (Adjusted $\underline{R}^2 = .27$ $\underline{p} < .001$). This is an acceptable proportion of explained variance considering the fact that only three predictor variables were included in the analysis. Again, the flow characteristics based on the eight-dimensional structure seems to show a slightly better sensitivity towards work motivation. The results are presented in table 7 as a comparison to the same analysis executed on the nine-dimensional flow structure above.

Table 7
Block regression for motivation

	Nine-dimensional flow structure				Eight-dimensional flow structure		
	Beta	t-value	F-change		Beta	t-value	F-change
Autotelic experience	.33***	4,5***	37,5***	Autotelic experience	.33***	4,7***	37,5***
Clear goals	.20**	2,7**	10,7***	Clear goals	.25**	3,4**	15,3***
Job satisfaction	.17*	2,3*	5,6*	Job satisfaction	.16*	2,3*	5,4*

N=164-170. *** = p< .001; ** = p< .01; * = p< .05
Adjusted $\underline{R}^2 = .25$

N=164-170. *** = p< .001; ** = p< .01; * = p< .05
Adjusted $\underline{R}^2 = .27$

3.4 Psychological flow and goal setting

Dimensional structure and reliability of goal setting. Principal Component Analysis was carried out on the goal setting inventory to explore dimensionality. As expected, the analysis suggested two factors out of the nine items, with one item loading ambiguously on both dimensions. A closer look on the factor loadings showed that the five items concerning organizational goals clustered together in the first dimension (factor loadings from .58 to .79). Chronbach's alpha was .79. The remaining three items, all concerning personal goal setting, clustered together with factor loadings varying from .68 to .79, and the Chronbach's alpha on this dimension was .62. Based on the theoretical foundation of the paper, only the personal goal dimension is interesting for further investigation.

Flow and goal setting. Four flow dimensions were significantly correlated to personal goal setting, i.e. clear goal, feedback, control, and the autotelic dimension. In addition, some of the flow dimensions were internally correlated, which made it unclear to what extent the correlations actually indicated a unique correspondence between the given flow dimension and personal goal setting (see table 4 and 5). These results applied to both the nine and the eight dimensional structures. In order to gain further information about the correspondence between flow and personal goal setting, two stepwise regression analysis were performed.

It was hypothesized that personal goal setting would contribute to increased frequency of flow. Consequently, the personal goal variable should be specified as the independent variable and the nine or eight flow dimensions as the dependent variables. However, this causality is difficult to test empirically due to the amount of dependent variables and only one independent variable. According to Davis (1985), it is acceptable to ignore causality in such situations. Therefore, direction of causality has not been considered when executing the analyses.

Nine dimensional flow structure. All together, the flow dimensions explained 24 % of the variance in personal goal setting (Adjusted $\underline{R}^2$ = .24 $\underline{p}$ < .001). Two of nine flow dimensions had a significant unique effect on personal goal setting. These were the autotelic experience dimension (beta = .36 $\underline{p}$ < .001) and the clear goal dimension (beta = .29 $\underline{p}$ < .001).

Eight dimensional flow structure. The flow dimensions of the eight dimensional model explained 26 % of the variance in personal goal setting (Adjusted $\underline{R}^2$ = .26 $\underline{p}$ < .001). Two flow dimensions had a significant unique effect on personal goal setting. These were the autotelic experience dimension (beta = .39 $\underline{p}$ < .001) and the clear goal dimension (beta = .32 $\underline{p}$ < .001).

4.0 Discussion

The first research inquiry of the present article was to explore reliability and consistency of the revised version of the Flow State Scale. The FSS was formerly developed to measure flow in sports settings, yet the present article assessed flow in work settings subsequent to rewriting some of the original items. Furthermore, it was interesting to investigate whether all dimensions were equally important to the flow experience in work activities as they have proven to be in other situations. Seven items failed to load correctly in the original nine-dimensional flow state scale (FSS) suggested by Jackson and Marsh (1996). Removing these seven items from the scale gave an eight-dimensional structure of flow with stronger and less ambiguous factor loadings, indicating a better fit to the data. All analyses of dimensionality showed that an eight-dimensional structure of the FSS was slightly better than the original nine-dimensional structure, although the differences were small.

Considering that some items were rewritten prior to the data collection process, it is not surprising that the original nine-dimensional structure was difficult to reconstruct. The changes suggested in the factor analysis may also be due to the nature of the items, as some may have been exclusively suited for sports settings. For instance, one item in the original time-alteration dimension asked if time progressed in "slow motion" while working on the given task. It is reasonable to believe that this applies to sports activities where time plays a crucial part to the performance. However, when working on a task where attention primarily is ruled by the person's cognitive capacity, time is more often experienced as going faster than usual (Larson, 1992). This item was one of the seven removed from the original nine-dimensional structure.

Overall, the results showed that the eight-dimensional structure consistently proved to be somewhat more sensitive towards work motivation. However, the differences were not substantial. It could be argued that the best option would be to keep the original form of the scale, considering the small differences between the two dimensional structures. Yet, it does not make sense to force variables into dimensions that does not go together due to its contents. Moreover, reliability analysis showed that the new model gave better alphas and demonstrated stronger internal validity than the original model. A thorough investigation of the two versions was thus necessary in order to avoid wrong and ambiguous findings.

The second hypothesis stated that flow experiences increase work motivation. This assumption was made on the basis of discoveries made in sports and educational research, presuming that the same would apply to work activities. The effect of flow on work motivation was tested through a comparison of the two FSS on work motivation. Interestingly, only two dimensions were significantly related to work motivation, namely the clear goal and the autotelic dimension. This was a consistent finding on all analyses using both the nine and the eight-dimensional structure. These results may indicate that only two dimensions of flow are of importance in work settings, contrary to the nine dimensions found to be important in sports activities (e.g., Jackson & Marsh, 1996).

It is interesting that none of the immediate experiential characteristics of flow proved to be significantly related to work motivation. One explanation could be that it is easier for respondents to recall the prerequisites and subsequent characteristics of the flow state when asked to think of a flow experience. Due to the core characteristics of flow, it follows that the state is very difficult to measure. Flow may be extremely intense at the moment of presence, yet the intensity fades away immediately after leaving the flow state. In the present study, flow was measured retrospectively, asking respondents to recall a flow incident before replying to the items. Consequently, the prerequisites and subsequent characteristics of flow, i.e clear goals and autotelic experience, may have been more easily accessible to memory. These were the two characteristics respondents most frequently graded as very high (see table 6b, percentage of experienced flow). Mark however that the three-dimensional categorization was made for the purpose of clarity by means of presenting the theory more readable, and has not been tested empirically.

Another reason why flow did not have such a strong impact on motivation as expected could be the motivation measurement. Although the dimensional structure of the motivation scale proved strong internal validity, it lacks inclusiveness as it consisted of only four items. Furthermore, the scale measured internal motivation only and would perhaps be more comprehensive if external motivation had been included. Recall that Kowal and Fortier (1999) claimed that research on the relation between internal and external motivation and psychological flow were ambiguous. Some studies did find that flow was significantly related to both internal and external motivation (e.g., Hills, Argyle & Reeves, 2000; Kowal & Fortier, 1999). However, if external motivation were to be included, direction of causality would have to be reversed. The present hypothesis stated that flow would increase motivation, and flow cannot increase external motivation, almost by definition. Yet, both internal and external motivation may increase flow, which ought to be tested in future studies.

The third main research issue was to empirically test the relation between goal setting and flow. Based on a theoretical analysis of goal setting effects, it was hypothesized that goal setting would increase occurrences of the flow experience, provided that the rules for productive goal setting are followed. Two analyses were executed, the first tested goal setting in relation to the original model on flow, the second with the new eight-dimensional model on flow. Both analyses showed that only two flow dimensions were significantly related to goal setting, namely the autotelic and the clear goal dimension, the same two dimensions that were significantly related to work motivation. The eight-dimensional flow model however explained more variance in goal setting than the nine-dimensional structure.

Interestingly, the autotelic dimension was the strongest dimension related to goal setting in both analyses. Recall that the flow experience is described as autotelic because it is intrinsically rewarding. Flow function as positive reinforcement, motivating individuals to work on a task only for the sake of the experience it provides. Consequently, flow leaves the person feeling satisfied (Csikszentmihalyi 1997; Han, 1992; Kowal & Fortier, 1999). According to Locke and Latham (2002), goals serve as a reference standard for satisfaction versus dissatisfaction. Exceeding the goal provides increasing satisfaction as the positive discrepancy grows, and not reaching the goal creates increasing dissatisfaction as the negative discrepancy grows. As argued by Locke and Latham (2002, p. 709) "across trials, the more goal successes one has, the higher one's total satisfaction". Bear in mind that the autotelic dimension was defined to be the end result of being in flow (see section 1.1, the flow construct). A possible explanation why the autotelic dimension was the strongest related to goal setting may thus be that both serve as a reference standard for satisfaction.

Goal setting was also significantly related to the clear goal dimension of flow. Although similar in description, these variables are not the same. Recall the discussion of subconscious processes given previously. Goal setting theory explains the act of consciously defining goals prior to action, whereas the clear goal dimension of flow also elucidate how goals continuously help the person stay on track (Locke & Latham, 2002; Csikszentmihalyi, 1997). The link between goal setting and the flow dimension clear goal may thus be due to goal setting enabling the person to sustain clear goals that guide the person through the flow experience.

The present study has a number of limitations. The theoretical foundation on which the goal setting hypothesis was made is particularly difficult to test empirically. First, the suggested complementary use of goal setting theory and flow is far more comprehensive than what is empirically testable through the specifications of hypotheses and statistical analyses. Furthermore, flow is primarily ruled by subconscious processes which complicate the use of self-completing questionnaires. The participants have explained their experiences retrospectively, which decrease the potential of truly capturing the essence of the experience.

However, the aim of statistical analyses is to measure tendencies in groups of people, not the phenomenological essence of an experience. It is necessary to establish a thorough theoretical foundation of conceptual relations prior to testing it statistically. If this study can corroborate that there exists a significant link between the flow experience and goal setting, it might stimulate to further research and thus a contribution to organizational psychology has been made. As shown in the theoretical analysis of goal setting and flow, there exists a reasonable foundation to believe that goal setting in reality is stronger related to flow than what has been proved in the present article.

Another limitation is the psychometric implications associated with the flow construct, even though research has managed to conceptualize it. Flow is a mental state engaged without conscious participation by the person acting. Thus, the experience can only be described and measured retrospectively, which limits the opportunity of capturing the true feeling of flow. Even though the eight-dimensional structure of the flow state scale provided very good results on reliability, internal consistency and discriminant validity, it does not necessarily imply that the measurement instrument is good. A new approach to measuring flow has been suggested by Vitterso (1998), who agues that the flow simplex structure is a lot more sensitive to variations in flow than other quantitative measurement questionnaires. The flow simplex is made up of seven bipolar adjectives descriptive for the flow experience. A simplex analysis is based on the factor structure found in principal component analysis. For details on the psychometric foundation underlying the flow simplex, see Straume (2004b). The simplex is based on the notion that the quality of a flow experience is curvilinear. Since most statistical analyses are based on linear relations, it follows that such analyses cannot confine to curvilinear relations. Consequently, if flow is curvilinear in nature, the flow state scale may not have measured the true variations in the employees' experience of flow.

Another limitation in the present study is that the relation between goal setting, flow and work motivation has not been tested in previous studies. This implies that the experience so far is limited, and certain changes ought to be made if the study is to be replicated. First of all, further adjustments can be made on the new Flow State Scale in order to make it even more applicable to work settings. Second, the motivation scale should have included external motivation. Third, the goal setting inventory could also have been improved. The dimensional structure of goal setting was not as good as it could have been (alpha = .62). Locke and Latham (1992) have argued that goal setting is extremely difficult to test using questionnaires as opposed to experimental research where the goals can be assigned in advance. However, this was not possible to do in the present study. Furthermore, due to the inherent difficulties of running analysis with nine dependent variables and only one independent variable, direction of causality was not taken into account when executing regression analysis on goal setting and flow. Consequently, there is no empirical evidence for the assumed causality of goal setting influencing flow although a relation was proved. However, the theoretical analysis on which the goal setting hypothesis was based supports the supposed direction of causality.

One of the strengths of this study is the contribution made to organizational psychology. Although the relations between goal setting, flow, and work motivation was not as strong as expected, they still were significant. The results may be due to accurate observations. Another explanation may be that the results partly were generated on the basis of insufficient measurement scales. Either way, the theoretical analysis given prior to the testing of hypotheses suggests that goal setting, flow, and work motivation may be stronger related to each other than empirically proved in the present study.

All together, this study has provided information about the relationship between goal setting, flow, and motivation. Previous research has shown that goal setting is a functional technique applicable to increase work performance among employees (Locke, 1997; Locke & Latham, 2002). A contribution to these findings has been made in the present article. The theoretical analysis of goal setting and flow shows how goal setting may increase the flow experiences in work activities. This was partly supported in the empirical analyses, as the clear goal and the autotelic flow dimensions were significantly related to goal setting. Accordingly, results suggest that flow can be considered when attempting to develop organizational initiatives meant to increase motivation.

References

Arnold, J., Cooper, C. L. & Robertson, I. T. (1998). *Work psychology: Understanding human behaviour in the workplace*. Pearson Education Limited: Prentice Hall.

Audia, G., Kristof-Brown, A., Brown, K. G., & Locke, E.A., (1996). Relationship of goals and microlevel work processes to performance on a multipath manual task. *Journal of Applied Psychology 81*(5), 483-497.

Cameron, J., Banko, K. M., & Pierce, W. D. (2001). Pervasive negative effects of rewards on intrinsic motivation: The myth continues. *The Behavior Analyst, 24*, 1-44.

Csikszentmihalyi, M. (1975a). *Beyond boredom and anxiety*. San Francisco: Jossey-Bass.

Csikszentmihalyi, M. (1996). *Creativity: Flow and the psychology of discovery and invention*. New York: Harper Collins.

Csikszentmihalyi, M. (1997). *Finding flow. The psychology of engagement with everyday life*. New York: Basic Books.

Csikszentmihalyi, M. (2003). *Good business. Leadership, flow and the making of meaning*. London: Hodder and Stoughton.

Csikszentmihalyi, M., & Csikszentmihalyi, I. S. (1992). *Optimal experience: Psychological studies of flow in consciousness* (pp. 15-36). New York: Cambridge University Press.

Csikszentmihalyi, M. & LeFevre, J. (1989). Optimal experience in work and leisure. *Journal of Personality and Social Psychology 56(5)*, 815-822.

Csikszentmihalyi, M & Nakamura, J. (1999). Emerging goals and the self-regulation of behaviour. In RS Wyer jr (Ed). *Perspectives on behavioural self regulation* (pp. 107-118). Mahwah: N.J. Lawrence Erlbaum.

Davis, J. A. (1985). *The logic of causal order*. London: Sage.

Eckblad, G. (1981). *Schema theory: A conceptual framework of cognitive-motivational processes*. London: Academy Press.

Gustafsson, J. E. & Stahl, P. A. (2000). *STREAMS user's guide. Version 2.5 for Windows*. Mölndal, Sweden: Mulitvariate Ware.

Hackman, J. R. and Oldman, G. R. (1975). General job satisfactioin scale. In: Cook, J. D., Hepworthe, S. J., Wall, T. D. & Warr, P. B. (1981). *The experience of work: A compendium and review of 249 measures and their use.* London: Academic Press.

Han, S. (1992). The relationship between life satisfaction and flow in elderly korean immigrants. In M. Csikszentmihalyi & I. S. Csikszentmihalyi (Eds.). *Optimal experience*: *Psychological studies of flow in consciousness* (pp. 138-149). New York: Cambridge University Press.

Hills, P., Argyle, M., & Reeves, R. (2000). Individual differences in leisure satisfactions: An investigation of four theories of leisure motivation. *Personality and Individual Differences 28*, 763-779.

Jackson, S. A. & Marsh, H. W. (1996). Development and validation of a scale to measure optimal experience: The flow state scale. *Journal of Sport and Exercise Psychology, 18*, 17-35.

Jørskog, K. G. & Sörbom, D. (1993). *LISREL 8. Structural equation modelling with SIMPLIS command language.* Hillsdale NJ: Erlbaum.

Kowal, J. & Fortier, M. S. (1999). Motivational determinants of flow: Contributions from self-determination theory. *The Journal of Social Psychology 139(3)*, 355-368.

Larson, R. (1992). Flow in Writing. In M. Csikszentmihalyi & I. S. Csikszentmihalyi (Eds.). *Optimal experience: Psychological studies of flow in consciousness* (pp. 172-182). New York: Cambridge University Press.

Lawler, E. E. & Hall, D. T. (1970). Internal work motivation scale. In Cook, J. D., Hepworthe, S. J., Wall, T. D. & Warr, P. B. (1981). *The experience of work: A compendium and review of 249 measures and their use.* London: Academic Press.

LeFevre, J. (1992). Flow and the quality of experiences during work and leisure. In M. Csikszentmihalyi & I. S. Csikszentmihalyi (Eds.). *Optimal experience: Psychological studies of flow in consciousness* (pp. 307-319). New York: Cambridge University Press.

Locke, E. A. (1997). The motivation to work: What we know. In M. Maehr & P. Pintrich (Eds.), *Advances in Motivation and Achievement (10)*, 375-412. Greenwich, CT: JAI Press.

Locke, E. A. & Latham, G. P. (2002). Building a practically useful theory of goal setting and task motivation. *American Psychologist 59(9)*, 705-717.

Locke, E. A. & Latham, G. P. (1990). *A theory of goal setting and task performance.* USA: Prentice Hall.

Marr, A. J. (2001). In the Zone: A biobehavioral theory of the flow experience. *The Online Journal of Sport Psychology 31,* 1-7. Benecom Technologies Inc.

Massimini, F., Csikszentmihalyi, M. & Delle Fave, A. (1992). Flow and biocultural evolution. In M. Csikszentmihalyi & I. S. Csikszentmihalyi (Eds.). *Optimal experience: Psychological studies of flow in consciousness* (pp. 60-85). New York: Cambridge University Press.

Nakamura, J. (1992). Optimal experience and the uses of talent. In M. Csikszentmihalyi & I. S. Csikszentmihalyi (Eds.). *Optimal experience: Psychological studies of flow in consciousness* (pp. 319-327). New York: Cambridge University Press.

Nunnaly, J. C. (1978). *Psychometric theory.* New York: McGraw-Hill.

Porter, L. W., & Lawler, E. E. (1968). *Managerial attitudes and performance.* Homewood, IL: Irwin-Dorsey.

Straume, L. V. (2004b). Flow and its effects on work motivation, work performance, and job satisfaction. 2nd Article of Master Thesis in Psychology, NTNU. Unpublished material.

Vitterssø, J. (1998). *Happy people and wonderful experiences: Structure and predictors of subjective well-being.* Doctoral dissertation, University of Tromsø.

Flow and Its Effects on Work Motivation, Work Performance, and Job Satisfaction: The Flow Simplex Structure

2nd Article of Master Thesis in Psychology
Lisa Vivoll Straume

Department of Psychology, Norwegian University of Science and Technology
Trondheim, Norway
Spring 2004

Abstract

The flow simplex structure was tested against the total of four specific work situations, i.e. (1) being totally absorbed in the task at hand (flow), (2) not having enough time to finish a task, (3) having plenty of time to finish a task, and (4) not succeeding in reaching a set goal. The flow simplex structure unfolded by the present data was investigated in these four situations in relation to the employees' subjective experience of work performance, work motivation, and job satisfaction. It was further hypothesized that the flow situation would increase work performance, work motivation, and job satisfaction. Data was collected through a self-completing questionnaire survey. The sample consisted of 170 employees from 9 different organizations in the Municipality of middle Norway, representing occupations from technology, financial departments, medical business, social services, and salesmen. Results indicated that flow in work settings is primarily experienced as fun and interesting, and not as challenging as expected. Traditional views hold that flow is strongly determined by the match between challenges and skills. Employees high on work performance, work motivation, and job satisfaction perceives the flow situation to be pleasant, fun, and joyful, respectively. Most employees experienced the time pressure situation as uncomfortable and sad, and the plenty of time situation as easy. The unsuccessful situation did not have any strong relation to the flow simplex adjectives. In conclusion, the flow situation was strongly related to work performance, work motivation, and job satisfaction, indicating that flow is an important predictor of these work behavior characteristics.

1.0 Flow in work situations

The conditions of employees work performance, motivation, and satisfaction are important issues that have been devoted substantial attention within the research of organizational psychological (e.g., Arnold, Cooper & Robertson, 1998; Cook, Hepworthe, Wall, & Warr, 1981; Locke & Latham, 1990). Primarily, this research has focused on the conscious intentions and deliberate choices of employees, and not the mental processes that operate outside of conscious awareness and guidance. Because the flow theory concerns the subconscious motivational processes of the working mind, it may give an important contribution to the understanding of employee's performance, motivation and satisfaction.

Psychological flow is a state of deep absorption where the individual functions at his or her fullest capacity (Shernoff, Csikszentmihalyi, Schneider, & Shernoff, 2003). The flow state occurs naturally in all people, independent of age, gender, and education (Csikszentmihalyi, 1975a, 1997, 2003). Previous research has also proven flow to be an important contributor to motivation, satisfaction and performance (Jackson & Marsh, 1996; Jackson, Thomas, Marsh, & Smethurst, 2001; Larson, 1992; Shernoff et al., 2003). Based on these findings and the notion of a universal flow experience, a natural supposition would be that such effects of flow apply to work situations as well. This inquiry was partly confirmed in a recent study (see Straume, 2004a), which tested general occurrences of flow in work settings. As a continuance of this study, the present study aims at examining flow in four specific work situations. This may increase comprehension of how the flow state is related to work performance, work motivation, and job satisfaction.

1.1 Theoretical approaches to the flow concept

Two main theoretical perspectives of flow are applied in the present study when exploring the relation between flow and work motivation, work performance, and job satisfaction, namely Eckblad's (1981) scheme theory and Csikszentmihalyi's flow theory (1975a, 1997, 2003). Csikszentmihalyi's flow theory constitutes mainly descriptions of how the flow state is experienced. According to him, the flow state involves a fine balance between the challenges of a task and one's ability to meet with those challenges. It is a state of mind where you become one with what you are doing, where action and awareness merges into a unified process of total concentration. This causes the awareness of the self to disappear. Yet the absence of self-consciousness does not mean that the person is unaware of what is happening in mind or body, but rather is focusing on the activity. The sense of time alters, distorting the well known distinction between past, present, and future. Flow also requires clearly defined goals. As a reference standard to these goals, immediate and clear feedback is continuously received by the person. Finally, flow feels similar to an autotelic experience. Csikszentmihalyi (1997) describes this as the end result of being in flow, meaning that the experience is intrinsically rewarding. Consequently, flow function as positive reinforcement in that it motivates the person to work on a task for the joy of the experience itself, and not for any external rewards (Csikszentmihalyi, 1975a, 1997, 2003; Csikszentmihalyi & Nakamura, 1999; Jackson & Marsh, 1996; Kowal & Fortier, 1999).

The features of flow presented above serves to depict what flow is, and how it affects our experience of being totally absorbed in a task. However, the complex dynamic processes of cognition, emotion, and motivation in flow are not given attention. In an attempt to integrate these processes into a unifying theory of psychological flow, Eckblad (1981) uses scheme theory to gain the depth lacking in Csikszentmihalyi's description of flow. This is recognized by Csikszentmihalyi himself (1992). As argued by Vitterssø, Vorkinn, and Vistad, "Eckblads flow theory is an integration of plans, goals and representations into a dynamic theory of optimal experiences" (2001, p. 140). Although both theories are important contributions, Eckblad's approach is given the highest priority due to the substantial account of integrated processes and the empirical analysis executed in the present article. Most data on work situations was gathered using the flow simplex structure. The flow simplex is based on the notion of unfolding data, and draws heavily on Eckblad's scheme theory.

1.2 Conceptualizing flow through scheme theory
Eckblad's (1981) scheme theory is primarily inspired by process-oriented views associated with the philosophy of constructive alternativism in the Piagetian use of the term. This view holds that the organism is a system where one major integrated process is continuously operative. Flow occurs in this process, depending on what actions the organism undertakes. Schemes are seen as organized sequences of mental operations, functioning within a hierarchic system. Systems of schemes are constantly operative, but the particular scheme active will depend on the situation we encounter. Eckblad (1981) describes the systems of schemes as means-end structures. This implies that every scheme has a beginning and an end, although they are connected to other schemes. More specifically, "any scheme functions as a means in relation to the goals of subordinate schemes, and at the same time as an end or goal

for subordinate schemes" (Eckblad, 1981, p. 28). The structure of a scheme then is ordered, yet flexible to all types of behaviors within the organism.

Schemes continuously undergo adaptive changes through the processes of assimilation or accommodation. It is the ease of assimilation that determines how affective responses are experienced. Mark however that pure assimilations does not exist due to the dynamic nature of person-environment interactions. Hence, every event will be somewhat impeded in terms of assimilation (Vittersø, 2004). As an indicator of assimilation ease, Eckblad (1981) has introduced the notion of assimilation resistance (AR). The AR represents the discrepancy between an individual's cognitive knowledge and the perception of a given situation. It is the size of this discrepancy that determines the quality of the affective response to the given situation. Very low levels of AR is experienced as easy, advancing toward pleasant as the AR becomes somewhat larger. Furthermore, these experiences are replaced by affects such as interest and challenge as the AR increase. At very high AR levels, interest and challenge are turned into frustration and anxiety. The more complex a situation grows, the more will the discrepancy increase, ultimately leading to negative affect because the person perceives the situation to be impossible to conceive (Eckblad, 1981; Vittersø, 2004).

When a scheme fails to assimilate it enters a state of disequilibrium. This is a motivational state that causes awareness to become centered on its activity, driven by the desire to bring the scheme back to the equilibrium state (Eckblad, 1981). The motivational state is a process of accommodation. A scheme can either accommodate through the activation of other sub-schemes, or gradually breed a permanent change where former schemes differentiate into newer versions in order to adapt to a new situation. In either case, there is a continuous process of cognitive and motivational processes where schemes are activated to guide the person through a specific behavior. During a process of intrinsic motivation, a scheme in disequilibrium will be "spontaneously active". Awareness becomes extremely focused; it is perceived as absorbing by the person, and this is what induces the flow experience.

1.3 Empirically testing the flow state of assimilation resistance
The quality of an affective response, e.g. flow, can be assessed using a flow simplex structure (Vittersø, 1998). The flow simplex structure draws heavily on Eckblad's scheme theory, which accounts for a particular spectrum of affective responses. These responses are related to schematic activity at different levels of assimilation resistance during goal approaching

activities. Eckblad (1980) originally assessed assimilation resistance based on a curvex structure of four bipolar adjectives. These were "easy" (E) "pleasantness" (P), "interestingness" (I), and "difficultness" (D), so that E < P < I < D in terms of assimilation resistance. However, Vittersø (1998) provided evidence that the relation between affective experiences and assimilation resistance is a *simplex* structure, and not a curvex. He furthermore suggested to include adjectives such as enjoyableness, fun, and dramatic to be a part of the simplex structure.

The term simplex was first defined by Guttmann (1954) as a part of his theory of ordered factors. This theory is an alternative to the better-known theory of common factors. The principle behind a simplex refers to differences in the *degree* between variables belonging to a simple hierarchical organized dimension. The name "simplex" refers thus to a *sim*ple structure of com*plex*ity between variables *of the same dimension* (Vittersø, 1998; Vittersø et al., 2001).

The flow simplex is thus based on a rank order of assimilation resistance of "easy", "pleasant", "joy", "fun", "interest", "challenge", and "dramatic", which means that E < P < J < F < I < C < D. For each type of experience, the positive quality decreases after reaching a peak, which means that each variable is curvilieary related to AR. Hence, most statistical methods will fail to reproduce the true structure of these data simply because of the linear arithmetics inherent in these methods (Vittersø, 2004). This means that the hierarchical structure of a dimension cannot be reproduced by either common factor or principal component analysis. Nevertheless, if the data conform to the pattern of a simplex, it may be detected by inspection of the correlation matrix produced by the simplex variables (Vittersø, 2004; Vittersø et al., 2001). The prediction of an unfolding model can be made from a Principal Component Analysis (PCA) according to the following three propositions:

1. The stimulus x stimulus correlation matrix will display a simplex-like structure. A simplex structure is recognized in a correlation matrix if there exist a permutation of the rows and the columns such that the entries taper off from the highest values along the diagonal to the lowest values in the lower left corner. The columns totals in the matrix should be approximately curvilinear with the lowest values at the extremes of the tables and the maximum in the middle of the table.
2. If the stimulus k is intermediate to stimulus j and l in the ordering and if the product of correlations $r_{jk} r_{kl}$ is negative, then the partial correlation $r_{jl \cdot k}$ must be negative. If stimulus k is not intermediate to j and l and if $r_{jk} r_{kl}$ is positive, then $r_{jl \cdot k}$ must be positive.

3. Principal component analysis of the correlation matrix will yield a semicircular, two-factor structure. Along the semicircle, variables will be ordered by their positions on the stimulus dimension.

                (Davidson, 1977, pp. 533-24. See also Vittersø et al., 2001, p. 145)

Variable j and l represents the beginning and the end of the rank order, in this case "easy" and "dramatic". The intermediate variable k is presently represented vicariously as "pleasantness", "enjoyableness", "fun", "interest", and "challenge". Given that the above assumptions are met, a Principal Component Analysis (PCA) may be a useful tool in revealing relationships among variables underlying a single curvilinear dimension such as flow. The analysis will suggest two factors, but the extra factor produced should be interpreted according to the theory of unfolding data, and not as an ordinarily achieved orthogonal factor. However, both factors are meaningful to interpret as the first component of the PCA represents the original dimension, and the second component would be the vector of the median variable on this dimension (Vittersø, 1998, p. 100).

The flow simplex measurement has consistently proven to be more sensitive to variations in affective responses than regular multi-dimensional constructs and measurement questionnaires (Vittersø, 1998, 2003; Vittersø et al., 2001). Thus, measuring flow in specific situations using the flow simplex may detect internal variations in the affective responses associated with specific experiences. It is particularly interesting to investigate whether the flow state in work activities equals the flow state described by Csikszentmihalyi and Csikszentmihalyi (1992). Furthermore, the variables of the flow simplex may be useful when interpreting the relation between flow and work motivation, work performance, and job satisfaction.

1.4 Psychological flow and work motivation

Work motivation is presently defined in terms of the degree to which an employee is self-motivated to perform effectively. It refers to the extent to which he or she experiences positive feelings when doing well and negative reactions when working poorly (Hackman & Oldham, 1975). Csikszentmihalyi and LeFevre (1989) investigated flow occurrences in work and leisure settings. They found that "flow-like situations" (p. 818) occurred three times as often in work as in leisure, but that motivation responses in relation to flow were always higher on leisure than on work. However, motivation was in this context measured with the item "Did you wish you had been doing something else?" which might have been rather vague to account for work motivation in general. Yet, it nevertheless supports the idea of flow as a predictor of motivation.

The flow experience seems to be motivating in two manners. Firstly, flow provides an immediate and continuous motivation to stay on the task at hand. Perceived control, total involvement, and balance of challenges and skills constitute an inspiration to continue. The flow simplex analysis described introductory is particularly interesting to apply when testing the immediate motivational effects of being in flow, as it has proven to be especially sensitive to variations in affective responses. Secondly, flow itself is a reward for doing the activity (Marr, 2001). In both instances, behavior is driven by intrinsic motivation, i.e. without any reward other than that provided by the activity itself. Accordingly, two levels of motivation are tested in the present article, namely how employees that are high in motivation will experience the flow situation, and internal motivation to keep on working after experiencing flow in a given task.

1.5 Psychological flow and job satisfaction

Job satisfaction is presently understood as a general feeling an employee has towards his or her job. It has been argued that job satisfaction should be understood as a multidimensional construct, as employees can be satisfied with certain aspect of a job, yet dissatisfied with other aspects (Spector, 1996). However, the present study measures only one aspect, namely flow in a specific situation. Consequently, a construct that measure the general feeling of satisfaction related to the given situational experiences was used.

People who experience flow regularly report feeling more satisfied, more in control, and less dependent on external rewards (Csikszentmihalyi & LeFevre, 1989; Han, 1992; Kowal & Fortier, 1999). Satisfaction is manifested at two levels. First of all, the flow experience is often described as intensely pleasurable (Csikszentmihalyi, 1996). This may be due to the fact that flow involves a level of concentration that does not leave room for distractive thoughts. Thus, the flow state creates an off-zone for irrelevant inputs and emotional discomfort. Secondly, it makes sense to assume that aggregated experiences of satisfaction in turn will create a general sense of satisfaction. In fact, research has shown that flow deprivation causes tens and irritable mood, anxiety and symptoms of depression (Csikszentmihalyi, 1975a). Hence, it makes sense to assume that high levels of flow in work settings will lead to high levels of satisfaction at work. Consequently, it is hypothesized that psychological flow is a predictor of satisfaction both while in the flow state, and subsequent to a flow experience.

1.6 Psychological flow and work performance

Work performance as a concept covers a wide range of behavioral incentives. Production records, absenteeism, disciplinary, hours spent at work and lateness are just a few examples of how to objectively appraise the employees' performance. The flow state is presently approached through the subjective experience. Accordingly, the main interest is the employee's subjective experience of his or her own work performance in relation to flow. Work performance is presently used to depict increased efficiency as a consequence of high levels of motivation and flow. This further implies that work performance ought to be measured through self-evaluations. It has been argued that such self-evaluations of work performance may suffer a great deal of error due to the desire of self-enhancement (Festinger, 1954). However, Mabe and West (1982) examined articles on the ability of self-evaluations and concluded that people's ability to evaluate themselves closely corresponded to performance on criterion measures. Consequently, self-evaluation scales may be useful in measuring employees' ability to carry out their work tasks.

Unfortunately, few research studies, if any, have empirically tested how flow affects work performance. However, it is an interesting research inquiry as actions that induces flow increases the cognitive capacity (Csikszentmihalyi & LeFevre, 1989; Marr, 2001). Flow is focused attention, and focused attention implies that the person invest all his or her psychic energy in the task at hand (Jackson & Marsh, 2001; Csikszentmihalyi & Nakamura, 1999). Flow is often referred to as peak performance, indicating a sense of optimal utilization of ones abilities. Jackson and Marsh (2001) have argued that assessments of flow tied to specific performances are important to obtain, although the authors refer to the relation between flow and performance in sports settings. It makes sense to assume that employees would appraise their own performance as being better when in flow, as opposed to being bored, anxious, or apathetic.

1.7 Aims of the paper

Overall, the primary aim of the paper is to test the flow simplex variables in four specific situations at work. In order to capture the flow state as accurate as possible, the first situation asked respondents to recall a situation at work in which they experienced being completely absorbed in the task at hand. Even though psychological flow was of primary interest, three more situations were added in order to appraise differences. Since a regular work day is often characterized of time-based pressure, two of the situations added concerned time spent on a work task. Consequently, one situation asked respondents to recall an incident where they felt stressed out on time and had to finish an important task, the other where they had plenty of time to finish a given task. It was interesting to investigate how being short on time as opposed to having plenty of time would relate to the order of the flow simplex variables. Furthermore, since flow often is experienced as being in control and of doing the right things, the last and fourth situation concerned not succeeding in reaching a set goal to trace potential differences. The situation was written down and then graded on the flow simplex items, following measures on work performance, work motivation, and job satisfaction. This procedure applied to all four situations measured. Based on the above assumptions, the following specific research questions constitute the present article:

1. The first research aim is to investigate whether the data confirm to the flow simplex structure, furthermore enabling the specific hypotheses of the article to be tested in relation to a simplex structure of flow.
2. The first flow-simplex situation in the questionnaire asked respondents to recall an incident of being totally absorbed in the task at hand. It is hypothesized that this situation is representative for Csikszentmihalyi's definition of the flow state, i.e. that it is perceived as interesting and challenging. Furthermore, such a situation is believed to increase the employees' motivation, satisfaction and work performance, both while in the flow state, and after the flow state has occurred.
3. The second flow-simplex situation asked respondents to think of a situation in which they felt really stressed out on time yet had to finish the task at hand. No theoretical foundation exists to hypothesize how such a situation is perceived in relation to the flow structure, work motivation, work performance and job satisfaction. It was generally interesting to gain information about how this situation would turn out.
4. The third situation asked respondents to think of a situation in which they had plenty of time to finish the task at hand. Missing theoretical foundation for specification of hypothesis applies for this situation as well. Accordingly, the empirical analyses aimed at exploring how such a situation relates to the flow-simplex variables, work motivation, work performance, and job satisfaction.

5. The fourth situation concerned not succeeding in reaching an important goal of a work task. The primary interest was to investigate how such a situation relates to the flow-simplex variables and work performance, work motivation, and job satisfaction.
6. The final specific aim of the paper was to examine the subsequent effects of the four situations. It is hypothesized that the flow situation will be the most important experience in relation to high levels of work performance, work motivation, and job satisfaction.

2.0 Method

2.1 Sample

Participants in the present study were 170 employees from 9 different organizations in Norway. The sample represented occupations from technology, financial departments, medical business, social services, and salesmen. Initially, 12 different organizations were invited to participate in the present study. All were selected from the list of customers in a consulting company in the Municipality of Trondheim, which is located in the middle part of Norway. Data were gathered by means of a questionnaire, distributed to employees by executives in daily charge at each work place. The respondent returned the questionnaire in a box located at each work place. All the attendants were informed in advance that the data will be treated confidentially.

Of the 400 questionnaires distributed, 170 were returned, which gives a response rate of 42,5 %. 78 were women and 91 were men, and one participant did not specify gender. Average age of the group was 38 years (SD = 9.0), 54 % had university education, and 96 % worked full time.

2.2 Questionnaire

The questionnaire originally consisted of two parts. The first part measured general occurrences of psychological flow, work motivation, job satisfaction, work performance, goal setting and openness to experience. Only a restricted proportion of the general part was used in the present study to measure general occurrences of flow (see Straume, 2004a). The second part measured the flow experience in specific situations, where respondent were asked to recall four different types of situations and then grade their flow experience on a flow simplex structure. This part of the questionnaire also contained items on motivation, satisfaction and work performance related to the specific flow instance. The specific part was of primary interest in the present study. However, some analyses did include parts of the flow measures from the general part.

Demographic and Work Characteristics. Personal demographic variables included year of birth, gender, marital status, and education. The work characteristics included the present work situation, number of years engaged in the occupation, tenure in the present position, work hours during a week, and overtime hours a week.

Flow State Scale. An eight-dimensional scale consisting of 29 items was used to measure level and intensity of the flow experience in general. Flow was assessed on a 5-point Likert scale ranging from strongly disagree to strongly agree. The scale was originally developed by Jackson and Marsh (1996) to measure flow in sport and physical activity settings, consisting of 36 items and nine dimensions. However, a revised version of the scale was used in order to gather data on flow in work settings. For details on this procedure and analysis of dimensionality, see Straume (2004a).

Before responding to the flow state scale, respondents were asked to recall a specific situation at work where they experienced being totally absorbed in a task. In order to more easily keep in mind the flow experience, respondents were asked to write down the situation they were thinking of.

Flow simplex structure. The flow simplex structure is developed by Eckblad (1981) and refined by Vittersø (1998) and was used to assess flow in specific situations. The flow simplex measurement is made up of seven adjectives that characterize the flow state. The adjectives are termed on a semantic differential scale, and subjects responded to a seven-point scale listed between the binary adjectives. The flow adjectives were easy-difficult, pleasant-unpleasant, joyful-sad, funny-boring, interesting-uninteresting, challenging-tame, and dramatic-undramatic.

Four specific situations were assessed using the flow simplex structure. These were (1) being totally absorbed and engaged in a task, (2) being very short on time to finish a task, (3) having more time than needed to finish a task, and (4) not succeeding in reaching a set goal. Respondents were asked to recall an instance of the given situation, and write down this situation in provided areas. After responding to the flow simplex structure following a specific situation, four items measuring work performance, work motivation and job satisfaction followed. The entire questionnaire is presented in Appendix B.

2.3 Statistical analyses

Principal Component Analysis using a chain P-technique was executed to unfold the data of the flow simplex. Group mean differences of factor scores for employees high and low in the variables work performance, work motivation, and job satisfaction were examined by means of t-tests. Multivariate analysis of variance (MANOVA) was applied to analyze differences between the flow dimensions defined by Csikszentmihalyi and the demographic variables. MANOVA was also used to measure whether or not there was an overall effect of the four situations on work performance, work motivation, and job satisfaction. One-way analysis of variance (ANOVA) using Bonferroni Post Hoc comparisons tested each of the dependent variables work performance, work motivation, and job satisfaction in relation to the four situations.

3.0 Results

3.1 The flow experience

Mean, standard deviation, and percentage of general flow experiences at work is presented in table 1. The results in this table are based on an eight-dimensional structure of the flow state (see Straume, 2004a for further details). The data represents the characteristics suggested by Jackson and Marsh (1996) and Csikszentmihalyi (1997).

Table 1. Percentage of experienced flow based on 8 dimensions

Dimension of FSS	Very High	High	Medium	Low	M	SD
1. Challenge / skill	13 %	60 %	20 %	7 %	4,0	.70
2. Merging self / act.	6 %	18 %	36 %	44 %	3,0	.84
3. Clear goals	26 %	52 %	19 %	2 %	4,1	.69
4. Feedback / control	6 %	45 %	48 %	6 %	3,8	.54
5. Concentration	12 %	65 %	21 %	1 %	4,1	.56
6. Loss of self-cons	3 %	38 %	36 %	23 %	3,5	.85
7. Time alteration	3 %	23 %	52 %	23 %	3,3	.77
8. Autotelic	13 %	55 %	28 %	4 %	4,1	.61

Note. N = 164-170

Multivariate analysis of variance (MANOVA) was applied to test if there were significant differences between flow and demographic variables. MANOVA tests the overall effects of the independent variables, allowing several criteria variables to be included. This reduces the probability of Type I errors. Additionally, the MANOVA-estimates analyze the association between the criterion variables, which in this particular analysis are the eight flow dimensions. The MANOVA analysis was carried out computing the eight dimensions of flow as dependent variables, and gender, age, marital status, years of education and type of education as independent variables. None of the variables had an overall significant effect on the flow experience. Accordingly, it was not profitable to make any further analysis. The results were in line with Csikszentmihalyi's flow theory which states that frequency and intensity of experienced flow does not depend on a person's demographic characteristics.

3.2 The flow simplex structure in four work situations

A chain P-technique was used to test whether the three propositions presented above were fulfilled for the present data (Cattell, 1973). The correlation matrix derived from the chain-P matrix revealed a simplex-like pattern. There was a clear tendency for the correlations to taper off from the highest values along the diagonal to the lowest values in the left bottom corner in the matrices (see Appendix A) (Vittersø, 2004).

Results are presented as plots of the flow simplex structure in figures 1-5. The arrangement of the seven flow adjectives in the plot represents how the present data unfolded. The adjectives of the flow-simplex are ordered according to their positions on the assimilation resistance dimension, exactly as expected by means of $E < P < J < F < I < C < D$. The two first principal components (factors) explained a total variance of 73.3 %, and the results are entirely in line with the underlying assumption of a flow simplex. Recall that although the plots consist of a two-factor structure, it should be interpreted as one dimension as the second dimension only is an artifact due to the factor analytic (i.e. linear) treatment of a curvilinear data structure. The first plot reveals the mean factor score for each situation (Figure 1), the next four plots (figures 2-5) show the correlation coefficients between the factor scores of the situation and work performance, work motivation, and job satisfaction.

3.2.1 Flow simplex in four situations

Figure 1 shows the mean factor scores of each situation in the flow-simplex structure. The black spot "flow" represents the situation where respondents were asked to recall an incident of being totally absorbed in a task. Concretely, this point reflects the mean factor scores of factor one (the axis) and factor two (y-axis) for the absorbed situation. As can be read from the plot, subjects experienced this as being fun and interesting. The right-skewed spot (time pressure) represents the situation where respondents were asked to recall an incident of not having enough time to fulfill a task. Interestingly, this situation is placed between the opposite axis of joy and fun. Relative to the other situations, the time pressure is experienced as rather unpleasant. This indicates that most respondents experience working under time-based pressure as some place between sad, boring, and uncomfortable. The left-skewed spot represents the situation of having plenty of time to finish a given task. As seen in Figure 1, this situation is located close to easy, indicating that this type of situation does not involve challenges or difficulty. Finally, the situation of not succeeding in reaching a goal is represented by the white spot.

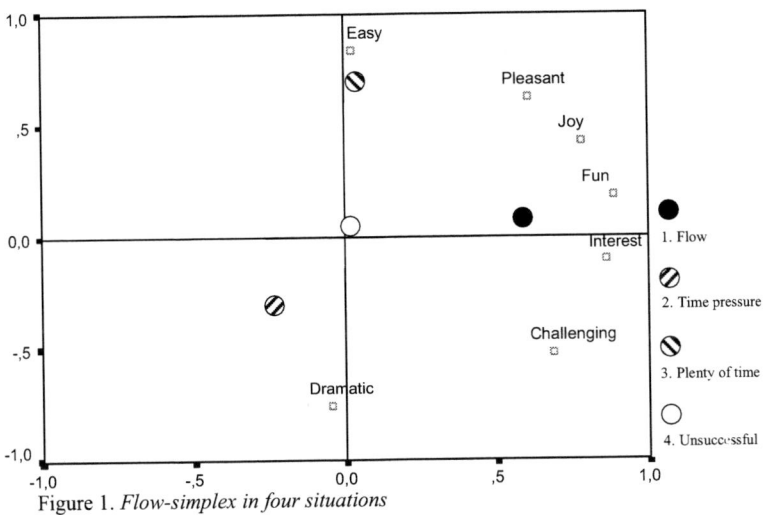

Figure 1. *Flow-simplex in four situations*

3.2.2 The experience of being in flow at work

Figure 2 shows how work performance, work motivation, and job satisfaction is experienced when the person is in flow. The three variables are located in the configuration according to the mean factor scores for groups high (circles) or low (squares) on the three independent variables. As can be read from the figure, work performance, work motivation and job satisfaction all varies along the joy/fun dimension in the plot ($M_{WPH} = 0.78$, $M_{WPL} = 0.006$ on factor 1, $t = -3.1$, $p < .01$ and $M_{WPH} = 0.15$, $M_{WPL} = -0.25$ on factor 2, $t = -1.3$, ns; $M_{WMH} =$

0.81, M_{WML} = -0.34 on factor 1, t = -5.5, p < .001 and M_{WMH} = 0.15, M_{WML} = -0.49 on factor 2, t = -1.3, p < .05; M_{JSH} = 0.80, M_{JSPL} = -0.008 on factor 1, t = -3.9, p < .001 and M_{JSPH} = 0.15, M_{JSL} = -0.34 on factor 2, t = -1.95, p = .05). The results indicate that those high on work performance, work motivation and job satisfaction will primarily experience flow as fun and joyful.

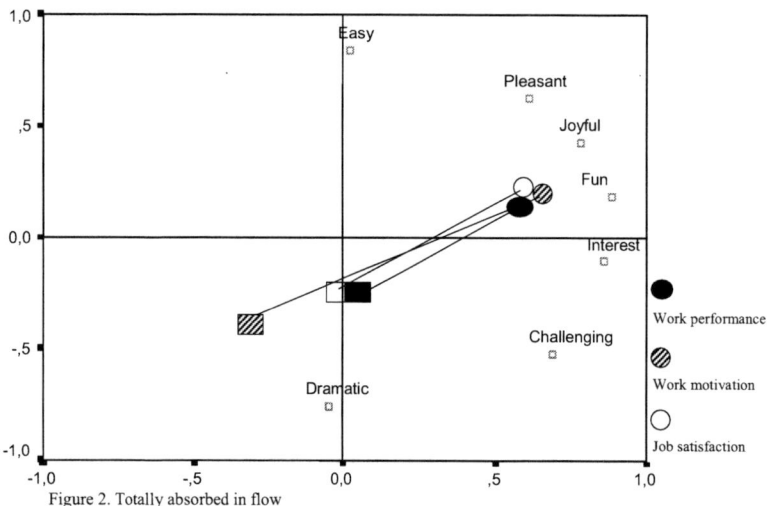

Figure 2. Totally absorbed in flow

3.2.3 The experience of not having enough time to finish a work task

Figure 3 shows how work performance, work motivation, and job satisfaction is perceived on the flow-dimension when time pressure is high. Work performance and job satisfaction are still differentiated along the joy/fun dimension, whereas the difference between individuals high and low on work motivation moved toward a difference in experiencing the situation as challenging. (M_{WPH} = 0.07, M_{WPL} = 0.72 on factor 1, t = -4.4, p < .001 and M_{WPH} = -0.32, M_{WPL} = -0.45 on factor 2, t = -0.83, ns; M_{WMH} = 0.08, M_{WML} = -0.01 on factor 1, t = -8.5, p < .001 and M_{WMH} = -0.46, M_{WML} = -0.12 on factor 2, t = -2.9, p < .05; M_{JSH} = 0.06, M_{JSPL} = -0.82 on factor 1, t = -5.14, p < .001 and M_{JSPH} = 0.32, M_{JSL} = -0.45 on factor 2, t = -0.77, ns.).

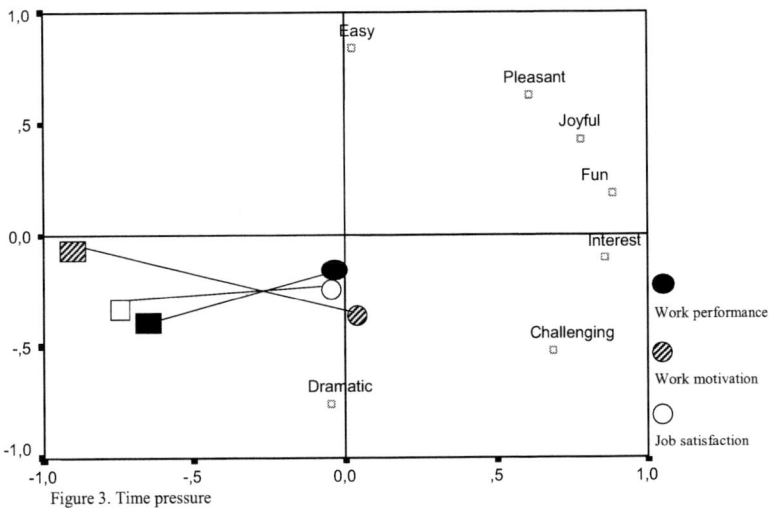

Figure 3. Time pressure

3.2.4 The experience of having plenty of time to finish a work task

The plenty of time-situation shows that work motivation and job satisfaction basically differs along the interesting dimension (although still being perceived as easy), whereas the difference on work performance is somewhat more oriented along the pleasant –unpleasant dimension ($M_{WPH} = 0.18$, $M_{WPL} = -1.1$ on factor 1, $t = -5.5$, $p < .001$ and $M_{WPH} = .84$, $M_{WPL} = 0.43$ on factor 2, $t = -2.19$, $p < .05$; $M_{WMH} = 0.46$, $M_{WML} = -1.13$ on factor 1, $t = -10.56$, $p < .001$ and $M_{WMH} = 0.71$, $M_{WML} = 0.96$ on factor 2, $t = 1.72$, ns.; $M_{JSH} = 0.30$, $M_{JSPL} = -1.46$ on factor 1, $t = -9.14$, $p < .001$ and $M_{JSPH} = 0.76$, $M_{JSL} = 0.87$ on factor 2, $t = 0.62$, ns.).

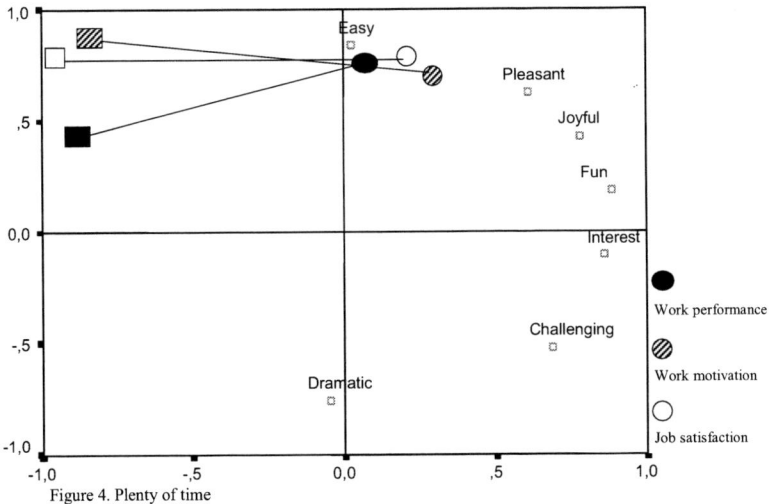

Figure 4. Plenty of time

3.2.5 The experience of not reaching a set goal at work

The analysis shows that those who managed to stay high on work performance perceived this situation to be more fun than employees low on this variable. Highly motivated individuals described the situation as more dramatic and challenging compared with their low motivated counterparts, and those satisfied where more pleased with the situation than those dissatisfied. (M_{WPH} = 0.23, M_{WPL} = -0.68 on factor 1, t = -5.4, p < .001 and M_{WPH} = -0.22, M_{WPL} = -0.62 on factor 2, t = -2.02, p < .05; M_{WMH} = -0.14, M_{WML} = -0.95 on factor 1, t = -6.87, p < .001 and M_{WMH} = -0.67, M_{WML} = -0.42 on factor 2, t = 1.80, ns.; M_{JSH} = -0.17, M_{JSPL} = -0.60 on factor 1, t = -2.131, p < .05 and M_{JSPH} = 0.02, M_{JSL} = -0.69 on factor 2, t = -3.60, p < .001). Results are presented in Figure 5.

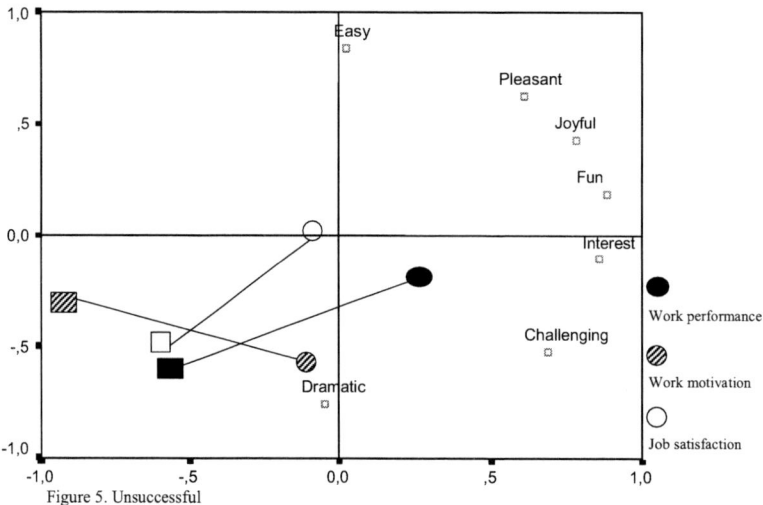

Figure 5. Unsuccessful

All four situations taken together, those high on work performance tended to perceive all situations to be more fun and interesting compared with those low on work performance. Work motivation operated in a somewhat similar manner, but differed during time pressure and unsuccessful task performance. Being highly motivated means to experience these situations as more challenging and dramatic. Job satisfaction follows the pattern of experiences revealed for work performance, except that being satisfied during an unsuccessful task means to feel more pleasant whereas work performance means to feel more interested. These results are especially interesting considering the fact that Csikszentmihalyi's flow theory is based on the experience of interest and challenge. Job satisfaction was located towards pleasant and joyful in the flow situation and the unsuccessful situation, and towards interestingness in both time situations.

3.3 Experiential effects of four situations

Table 1 shows the differences in work performance, work motivation, and job satisfaction in the four different situations. The range of score values varies between 1.0 which indicates low performance, motivation and satisfaction, and 5.0, indicating high levels. As can be seen, work performance as well as motivation and satisfaction were highest in the flow situation (mean score 4.2, 4.4, and 4.3, respectively). In the unsuccessful situation, these characteristics were the lowest (2.8, 3.3, and 2.6, respectively).

Table 1.
Differences in four situations due to work performance, work motivation, and job satisfaction

	Situation	Mean	SD	F
Work Performance	Flow	4,2	,62	
	Time pressure	3,8	,66	
	Plenty of time	4,1	,67	
	Unsuccessful	2,8	,78	
	Total	3,7	,88	138,3***
Work Motivation	Flow	4,4	,68	
	Time pressure	3,7	,80	
	Plenty of time	3,8	,86	
	Unsuccessful	3,3	,94	
	Total	3,8	,90	43,9***
Job Satisfaction	Flow	4,3	,69	
	Time pressure	3,8	,74	
	Plenty of time	4,0	,68	
	Unsuccessful	2,6	,88	
	Total	3,7	,99	157,8***

Note: N = 164-170. *** = $p < .001$; Roy's Largest Root = .911

Multivariate analysis of variance (MANOVA) was carried out in order to examine whether or not there was an overall effect of the four situations on the three dependent variables, i.e. work performance, work motivation, and job satisfaction. This also made it possible to analyze associations between the three dependent variables. These results showed that there was an overall significant effect (Roy's Largest Root = .911; F = 191.3, $p < .001$).

Due to the overall effect, the next step was to carry out one-way analysis of variance (ANOVA), one for each of the dependent variables. It was hypothesized that employees would experience more work performance, more work motivation and more job satisfaction after a flow experience than after the remaining three situations. Results showed that performance, motivation, and satisfaction were significantly higher in the flow situation than in the remaining three situations, i.e. work performance ($F = 138.3, p < .001$), work motivation ($F = 43.9, p < .001$) and job satisfaction ($F = 157.8, p < .001$) (see table 1).

To test how work performance, work motivation, and job satisfaction differed across situations, Bonferroni Post Hoc correction was carried out. Concerning work performance, all situations were significantly different except between the flow situation and the plenty of time situation. This indicates that employees appraise their work performance as almost equally high when they have plenty of time to finish a work task as in the flow situation. However, work performance is higher in flow than under time pressure and when they do not succeed in reaching a set goal. Work motivation differed significantly across all situations except between the time pressure and the plenty of time situation. These results indicate that levels of motivation remains the same independent of how much time the employees have available on a work task. The same applied for job satisfaction, where all differences between situations were significant, except between the time pressure and the plenty of time situation. All results are presented in table 2.

Table 2.
Differences between the four situations. Results of Bonferroni Post Hoc Correction

	Flow	Time pressure	Plenty of time
Work Performance			
Time pressure	$p < .001$		
Plenty of time	$p = ns$	$p < .001$	
Unsuccessful	$p < .001$	$p < .001$	$p < .001$
Work Motivation			
Time pressure	$p < .001$		
Plenty of time	$p < .001$	$p = ns$	
Unsuccessful	$p < .001$	$p < .001$	$p < .001$
Job Satisfaction			
Time pressure	$p < .001$		
Plenty of time	$p < .01$	$p = ns$	
Unsuccessful	$p < .001$	$p < .001$	$p < .001$

Note: N = 164-170; ns = non significant.

4.0 Discussion

The present data unfolded entirely to the notion of a flow simplex structure. Accordingly, the first specific hypothesis of the present article was to test whether the situation of being totally absorbed in the task at hand was representative for Csikszentmihalyi's definition of the flow state. Recall that according to Csikszentmihalyi, the task needs to be challenging in order for flow to occur (e.g., 1975a, 1997, 2003). The analysis of the four situations showed that flow in work settings was perceived as being some place between fun and interesting, and not as challenging as expected. Yet, most research based on Csikszentmihalyi's approach to flow has been conducted on sports and leisure activities, so these results could mean that the kind of flow employees experience at work is slightly different from the flow experience in leisure and sports settings. A possible explanation of this difference may be that people more easily can adjust the level of challenge in leisure or sport as their abilities increase. In work settings, challenges are not that easy to adjust purposively. Furthermore, most work tasks are not perceived as taxing when employees have considerable knowledge about how to solve the task. The absence of challenges does not necessarily prevent individuals to enter flow, but rather that flow is restricted to occur within the range of "potential challenges". Hence, flow is more often characterized as fun and joyful at work. Csikszentmihalyi (1996, 2003) have argued that challenges are important characteristic of flow in work situations too, but these findings were primarily based on interviews of executive leaders. Perhaps managers are faced with more challenges than other employees due to the core characteristics of their tenure. Research in organizational psychology has long appraised the role of autonomy as an important criterion of motivation, work performance, and job satisfaction (Arnold et al., 1998; Kaufmann & Kaufmann, 1998). These results may possibly indicate that autonomy is a predictor that also may facilitate the flow experience in work activities. Future research should include autonomy as a predictor of flow in order to empirically test this possible relation.

Another explanation for the difference between Csikszentmihalyi's definition of flow and the one detected here might be memory bias of self-reporting questionnaires. An individual's account for his or her emotional experiences can be biased in various ways (Thomas & Diener, 1990). Recalling subjective experiences involves reconstructions (e.g., Singer & Salovey, 1993) and at least some studies show that events are remembered more positively than original accounts (Vitterso, personal communication, 24. May, 2004). Other studies conclude differently (see Baumeister, Bratslavsky, & Finkenauer, 2001, for an overview), thus the precise nature of memory bias remains to be determined. Nevertheless, a growing body of studies have documented that affective experience are differently reported in real-time as compared with in retrospect (e.g., Kahneman, 1999), and this effect may account for some of the results reported in the current study.

It was also of interest to investigate how work performance, work motivation, and job satisfaction was experienced in the four different situations at work. On average, participants perceived the time pressure situation to be uncomfortable and sad and the plenty of time situation to be easy. Nevertheless, those high on work performance experienced both the flow situation and the plenty of time situation to be pleasant, and the unsuccessful situation to be vicariously pleasant and joyful, relative to those low in work performance. Contrary, the time pressure situation was located closer to the fun variable, indicating that this situation implied an increase in assimilation resistance. This means that the time pressure situation involved higher challenges than both flow, plenty of time, and unsuccessful. When employees are short on time, they are forced to work harder in order to make the deadline, which is experienced as more demanding than being sufficient on time. However, this may also help to focus attention and enhance their performance on the necessary work tasks. Although most employees experienced the time pressure situation as distressing, those high on work performance had experiences closer to interesting than those with low scores on this variable.

Interestingly, those high on motivation did not seem to perceive the task as less interesting if available time differed, or if they did not succeed in reaching a set goal. This is a strong indicator of the importance of being motivated at work, as being motivated seems to endure possible obstacles in work situations. Direction of causality was not tested in the present analysis, only the relation between the two variables. Perhaps there is a reversed effect between the two in that interest may be a predictor of motivation. Hence, the results may signify that if organizations manage to keep the work tasks interesting, employees will sustain motivation independent of being short on time or not reaching a set goal. However, more research in this area is needed before any conclusions can be drawn. Future studies should attempt to replicate these findings, and furthermore test the possible causal relations between motivation and interest in work situations based on the flow simplex.

Employees high in job satisfaction perceived both time situations to be pleasant and fun, relative to those low on satisfaction. The only difference was that the plenty of time situation increased slightly in degree of interest. These results may imply that those high in job satisfaction will continue to view their work as interesting independent of time-based pressure, which also was the case for work motivation. In view of these findings, the primary focus of organizational initiatives aimed at increasing motivation and satisfaction should perhaps be to keep the work tasks interesting rather than to protect employees from time pressure. This implies that we have to detect what conditions that needs to be present in order for employees to view their work tasks as interesting. The flow experience was also located between fun and interesting, and this might be a relation worth investigating. These results lead us into new appealing research questions that ought to be further investigated, namely whether interesting work tasks may contribute to increased work motivation, job satisfaction, and flow experiences.

The final specific aim of the paper was to investigate the subsequent effects of the four work situations tested. It was hypothesized that work performance, work motivation, and job satisfaction would be highest in the flow situation. This hypothesis was supported in the analyses. The flow situation, following the plenty of time situation, proved the highest mean scores in work performance, work motivation, and job satisfaction. These results show that when employees are deeply absorbed in the task at hand, they are left feeling more motivated, more satisfied, and more efficient than in situations where they are short on time or when they do not reach a set goal. Accordingly, flow experiences at work seem to be an important contributor to the employees' experience of their own performance, motivation, and satisfaction.

The results discussed above regarding the effects of flow in work situations are encouraging, yet they need to be interpreted in terms of the limitations imposed by the research approach taken. Firstly, these results alone are not sufficient to conclude that flow situations always will contribute to increased levels of work motivation, work performance, and job satisfaction. Future studies should try to replicate the findings, and especially analyze the potential differences between the subjective experience of work performance and objective appraisals of the employees' performance. The strength of the findings is dependent on the validity of the self-reported responses provided. The retrospective nature of these responses could have been clouded by priming effects, memory biases, and other situational influences, particularly since responses are based on affective experiences. Additionally, the fact that only four specific situations were investigated limits the potential of generalizing the findings. Future studies should try to include other situations that influence how employees perceive their work. Team-work, role of autonomy, organizational commitment, attitudes, and stress are just a few aspects that may influence the employees' perception of their work place and their role in it.

Despite these shortcomings, the present article has made a contribution to organizational psychology and the way in which we understand work behavior. Due to the core nature of human functioning, flow is an inevitable consequence of the working mind. The present study has provided information about potential effects of being in flow, and how interesting work tasks may be an important facilitator of work motivation and job satisfaction. Hopefully, a growing body of research on the relation between flow and work settings will characterize the future of organizational psychology, further expanding our knowledge of how the subconscious mind works.

References

Arnold, J., Cooper, C. L. & Robertson, I. T. (1998). *Work psychology: Understanding human behaviour in the workplace.* Pearson Education Limited: Prentice Hall.

Baumeister, R., Bratslavsky, E., & Finkenauer, C. (2001). Bad is stronger than good. *Review of General Psychology, 5,* 323-370.

Cattell, R. (1978). *The scientific use of factor analysis.* New York: Plenum Press.

Cook, J. D., Hepworthe, S. J., Wall, T. D., & Warr, P. B. (1981). *The experience of work: A compendium and review of 249 measures and their use.* London: Academic Press.

Csikszentmihalyi, M. (1975a). *Beyond boredom and anxiety.* San Francisco: Jossey-Bass.

Csikszentmihalyi, M. (1996). *Creativity: Flow and the psychology of discovery and invention.* New York: Harper Collins.

Csikszentmihalyi, M. (1997). *Finding flow. The psychology of engagement with everyday life.* New York: Basic Books.

Csikszentmihalyi, M. (2003). *Good business. Leadership, flow and the making of meaning.* London: Hodder and Stoughton.

Csikszentmihalyi, M. & Csikszentmihalyi, I. S. (1992). *Optimal experience: Psychological studies of flow in consciousness* (pp. 15-36). New York: Cambridge University Press.

Csikszentmihalyi, M. & LeFevre, J. (1989). Optimal experience in work and leisure. *Journal of Personality and Social Psychology 56*(5), 815-822.

Csikszentmihalyi, M. & Nakamura, J. (1999). Emerging goals and the self-regulation of behaviour. In RS Wyer jr (Ed). *Perspectives on behavioural self regulation* (pp. 107-118). Mahwah: N.J. Lawrence Erlbaum.

Davidson, M. L. (1977). On a metric, unidimensional unfolding model of attitudinal and developmental data. *Psychometrika, 42*(4), 523-548.

Eckblad, G. (1980). The curvex: Simple order structure revealed in ratings of complexity, interestingness, and pleasantness. *Scandinavian Journal of Psychology, 21,* 1-16.

Eckblad, G. (1981). *Schema theory: A conceptual framework of cognitive-motivational processes.* London: Academy Press.

Festinger, L. (1954). A theory of social comparison processes. *Human Relations, 7,* 117-140.

Guttman, L. (1954). A new approach to factor analysis: The radex. In P. F. Lazarsfeld (Ed.), *Mathematical thinking in the social sciences.* Glencoe: The Free Press. (Reissued New York: Russell & Russell, 1969).

Hackman, J. R. and Oldman, G. R. (1975). General job satisfactioin scale. In: Cook, J. D., Hepworthe, S. J., Wall, T. D. & Warr, P. B. (1981). *The experience of work: A compendium and review of 249 measures and their use*. London: Academic Press.

Han, S. (1992). The relationship between life satisfaction and flow in elderly korean immigrants. In M. Csikszentmihalyi & I. S. Csikszentmihalyi (Eds.). *Optimal experience: Psychological studies of flow in consciousness* (pp. 138-149). New York: Cambridge University Press.

Jackson, S. A. & Marsh, H. W. (1996). Development and validation of a scale to measure optimal experience: The flow state scale. *Journal of Sport and Exercise Psychology, 18*, 17-35.

Jackson, S. A., Thomas, P. R., Marsh, H. W., & Smethurst, C. J. (2001). Relationships between flow, self-concept, psychological skills, and performance. *Journal of Applied Sport Pscyhology, 13*, 129-153.

Kahneman, D. (1999). Objective happiness. In D. Kahneman, E. Diener, & N. Schwarz (Eds.), *Well-being: The foundations of hedonic psychology* (pp.3-25). New York: Russell Sage Foundation.

Kaufmann, G. & Kaufmann, A. (1998). *Psykologi i organisasjon og ledelse*. Bergen: Fagbokforlaget Vigmostad & Bjørke AS.

Kowal, J. & Fortier, M. S. (1999). Motivational determinants of flow: Contributions from self-determination theory. *The Journal of Social Psychology 139*(3), 355-368.

Larson, R. (1992). Flow in Writing. In M. Csikszentmihalyi & I. S. Csikszentmihalyi (Eds.). *Optimal experience: Psychological studies of flow in consciousness* (pp. 172-182). New York: Cambridge University Press.

Locke, E. A. & Latham, G. P. (1990). *A theory of goal setting and task performance*. USA: Prentice Hall.

Mabe, P. A., & West, S. G. (1982). Validity of self-evaluation of ability: A review and meta-analysis. *Journal of Applied Psychology, 67*, 280-296.

Marr, A. J. (2001). In the Zone: A biobehavioral theory of the flow experience. *The Online Journal of Sport Psychology 31,* 1-7. Benecom Technologies Inc.

Shernoff, D. J., Csikszentmihalyi, M., Schneider, B., & Shernoff, E. S. (2003). Student engagement in high school classrooms from the perspective of flow theory. *School Psychology Quarterly, 18*(2), 158-176.

Singer, J. A., & Salovey, P. (1993). The remembered self: Emotion and memory in personality. New York: The Free Press.

Spector, P. E. (1997). *Job satisfaction. Application, assessment, causes, and consequences.* California: Sage publications.

Straume, L. V. (2004a). *Flow in organizational psychology: A psychometric approach to the relations between goal setting, flow, and work motivation.* 1st Article of Master Thesis in Psychology, NTNU. Unpublished material.

Thomas, D. L. & Diener, E. (1990). Memory accuracy in the recall of emotions. *Journal of Personality and Social Psychology, 59*(2), 291-297.

Vittersø, J. (1998). *Happy people and wonderful experiences: Structure and predictors of subjective well-being.* Doctoral dissertation, University of Tromsø.

Vittersø, J. (2004). Subjective well-being versus self-actualization: Using the flow-simplex to promote a conceptual clarification of subjective quality of life. *Social Indicators Research, 65*, 299-331.s

Vittersø, J. & Kjøndahl, C. (2003). Measuring flow: Comparing three scales. Paper presented at *The 5th Conference of the International Society of Quality-of-Life Studies*, Frankfurt, Germany July 20-24.

Vittersø, J., Vorkinn, M., & Vistad, O. I. (2001). Congruence between recreational mode and actual behavior – a prerequisite for optimal experience. *Journal of Leisure Research, 33*(2), 137-159.

APPENDIX A

CORRELATION MATRIX FOR FLOW SIMPLEX VARIABLES

Correlation matrix for the Flow Simplex Variables

	1	2	3	4	5	6	7	$r_{jk}r_{kl}$	$r_{jl \cdot k}$
1. Easy	1,00	0,485	0,327	0,165	-0,032	-0,341	-0,436		
2. Pleasant	0,485	1,00	0,676	0,589	0,430	0,077	-0,396	-0,192	-0,306
3. Joyful	0,327	0,676	1,00	0,752	0,516	0,291	-0,319	-0,104	-0,373
4. Fun	0,165	0,589	0,752	1,00	0,674	0,429	-0,14	-0,024	-0,424
5. Interesting	-0,032	0,430	0,516	0,674	1,00	0,548	0,014	-0,001	-0,437
6. Challenging	-0,341	0,077	0,291	0,429	0,548	1,00	0,234	-0,080	-0,388
7. Dramatic	-0,436	-0,396	-0,319	-0,145	0,014	0,234	1,00		
	1,168	2,864	3,245	3,467	3,152	2,240	-0,047		

APPENDIX B

QUESTIONNAIRE

MOTIVASJON, TILFREDSHET OG PSYKOLOGISK FLYT I JOBBEN

SPØRREUNDERSØKELSE

Innledning

Formålet med denne undersøkelsen er å kartlegge hvordan opplevelsen av "psykologisk flyt" øker din motivasjon og tilfredshet i jobben. "Flyt" er den opplevelsen du har når du blir så engasjert av noe du holder på med at du blir helt oppslukt og "revet med". Ved å delta i denne undersøkelsen bidrar du til å øke vår kunnskap om hva som gjør jobben spennende og interessant.

Hvem står bak?

Spørreundersøkelsen gjennomføres av NTNU og Total Consult, og resultatene inngår i Lisa Vivoll Straumes hovedfagsoppgave i psykologi.

Konfidensialitet

All informasjon behandles konfidensielt. Når svarene skal analyseres vil ingen kunne se hvem som har svart.

Utfylling av skjemaet

Det er ingen riktige eller gale svar – det er dine oppriktige meninger vi er interessert i. Det er viktig at du besvarer alle spørsmålene. Det tar ca 15 minutter å fylle ut skjemaet.

Har du spørsmål om undersøkelsen kontakter du Lisa Vivoll Straume på lisavivo@stud.ntnu.no eller på tlf. 99 62 02 12.

På forhånd takk for hjelpen!

Husk: Bare ett kryss på hvert spørsmål!

	Skjemaet skal leses av en maskin. Følg derfor disse reglene:
LES DETTE FØR DU STARTER!	• Bruk svart/blå kulepenn, ikke tusj/svak blyant. Skriv tydelig, og ikke utenfor feltene. Bare feltene blir lest. • Sett bare ett kryss på hvert spørsmål, slik: ☒ *Feil kryss* • Krysser du feil, setter du nytt kryss på rett sted. Pass på at det rette krysset blir **kraftigst**, slik: ☒ ☒ • Ikke bruk overstryking når du skal korrigere feilkryssinger. Ved flere kryss på samme spørsmål regnes alltid det kraftigste som ditt svar *Korrigering* • Ikke brett arkene, og ikke kopier skjemaet. Bare originale skjema blir lest.

VIKTIG: IKKE FYLL UT SKJEMAET FØR DU HAR LEST INSTRUKSJONEN OVENFOR!

LITT OM DEG SELV

33. Kjønn:
    - Kvinne ☐₁
    - Mann ☐₂

34. Fødselsår: 19 ☐☐

35. Sivil status:
    - Enslig ☐₁
    - Gift eller samboende ☐₂
    - Separert eller skilt ☐₃
    - Enke eller enkemann ☐₄

36. Hva er din høyeste fullførte utdanning?
    - Grunnskole ☐₁
    - Gymnas/v.g.skole/yrkesskole ☐₂
    - Høgskole/universitet, inntil 3 år ☐₃
    - Høgskole/universitet, over 3 år ☐₄

37. Hvilken type utdanning har du?
    - Teknisk (realfag, ingeniør) ☐₁
    - Økonomisk/administrativ ☐₂
    - Samfunnsvitenskapelig ☐₂
    - Humanistisk ☐₄
    - Kunstnerisk ☐₅
    - Annen *(forklar⇩)* ☐₆

    Annen utdanning: *Bruk STORE, TYDELIGE BLOKKBOKSTAVER, og bare ett tegn i hvert felt)*

    ☐☐☐☐☐☐☐☐☐☐☐☐☐☐☐☐☐☐☐☐☐☐☐☐☐☐☐☐

38. Hvor mange år har du jobbet i denne bedriften?
    Avrund til nærmeste antall hele år. Mindre enn ett år avrundes oppover til 1 .... ☐☐ år

39. Hva slags ansettelsesforhold har du?   Fast ansatt ☐₁   Midlertidig eller vikariat ☐₂

40. Hvor mange timer er din "normalarbeidsuke"?
    Avrund til nærmeste antall hele timer. Regn ikke med pålagt overtid, "plusstimer", arbeid du tar med hjem etc .... ☐☐ timer/uke

41. Hvor mange timer "overtid" jobber du vanligvis pr. uke?
    Avrund til nærmeste antall hele timer. Regn med all tid utover normal arbeidstid; pålagt overtid, "plusstimer", arbeid du tar med hjem etc .... ☐☐ timer/uke

OPPLEVELSE AV PSYKOLOGISK FLYT

1. Tenk tilbake på en konkret situasjon i jobben da du ble engasjert og helt "oppslukt" av den oppgaven du gjorde. Beskriv kort hvilken arbeidsoppgave du tenker på:
   (*Bruk STORE, TYDELIGE BLOKKBOKSTAVER, og bare ett tegn i hvert felt*)

   ☐☐☐☐☐☐☐☐☐☐☐☐☐☐☐☐☐☐☐☐☐☐☐☐☐☐☐☐
   ☐☐☐☐☐☐☐☐☐☐☐☐☐☐☐☐☐☐☐☐☐☐☐☐☐☐☐☐

Før du fortsetter: Kontroller at du har svart på alle spørsmålene på denne sida!

Husk: Bare ett kryss på hvert spørsmål!

2. Hvordan opplevde du denne situasjonen?

	Svært uenig 1	Uenig 2	Verken /eller 3	Enig 4	Svært enig 5
1. Jeg ble utfordret, men jeg hadde tro på at mine kunnskaper gjorde meg i stand til å takle utfordringen	☐	☐	☐	☐	☐
2. Jeg tok de riktige valgene uten å tenke over hva jeg gjorde	☐	☐	☐	☐	☐
3. Jeg hadde en klar formening om hva jeg skulle gjøre	☐	☐	☐	☐	☐
4. Jeg hadde en klar oppfatning av at jeg gjorde det bra	☐	☐	☐	☐	☐
5. Min oppmerksomhet var utelukkende fokusert på det jeg holdt på med	☐	☐	☐	☐	☐
6. Jeg følte at jeg hadde full kontroll over det jeg gjorde	☐	☐	☐	☐	☐
7. Jeg var ikke opptatt av hva andre måtte tenke om meg	☐	☐	☐	☐	☐
8. Det virket som om tiden ble fordreid, enten til å gå fortere eller saktere enn vanlig	☐	☐	☐	☐	☐
9. Opplevelsen ga meg en veldig god følelse	☐	☐	☐	☐	☐
10. Mine kunnskaper sto i forhold til utfordringene i arbeidsoppgaven	☐	☐	☐	☐	☐
11. Ting lot bare til å skje automatisk	☐	☐	☐	☐	☐
12. Jeg hadde en sterk følelse av hva jeg skulle gjøre	☐	☐	☐	☐	☐
13. Jeg var klar over hvor godt jeg presterte	☐	☐	☐	☐	☐
14. Det var lett å konsentrere seg om det jeg gjorde	☐	☐	☐	☐	☐
15. Jeg følte jeg kunne kontrollere det jeg gjorde	☐	☐	☐	☐	☐
16. Jeg bekymret meg ikke over mine prestasjoner under oppgaven	☐	☐	☐	☐	☐
17. Måten tiden gikk på syntes å være annerledes enn ellers	☐	☐	☐	☐	☐
18. Jeg likte følelsen jeg fikk av prestasjonen, og ønsker å bli revet med av den igjen	☐	☐	☐	☐	☐
19. Jeg følte meg kompetent nok til å møte de vanskelige kravene i oppgaven	☐	☐	☐	☐	☐
20. Jeg presterte automatisk	☐	☐	☐	☐	☐
21. Jeg visste hva jeg ønsket å oppnå	☐	☐	☐	☐	☐
22. Mens jeg presterte hadde jeg en god ide om hvor godt jeg gjorde det	☐	☐	☐	☐	☐
23. Jeg var dypt konsentrert	☐	☐	☐	☐	☐
24. Jeg hadde en følelse av full kontroll	☐	☐	☐	☐	☐
25. Jeg var ikke opptatt av hvordan jeg framstilte meg selv	☐	☐	☐	☐	☐
26. Det føltes som om tiden stoppet opp mens jeg utførte handlingen	☐	☐	☐	☐	☐
27. Jeg satt igjen med en veldig god følelse	☐	☐	☐	☐	☐
28. Utfordringene og mine ferdigheter var på samme nivå	☐	☐	☐	☐	☐
29. Jeg handlet spontant og automatisk uten å behøve å tenke	☐	☐	☐	☐	☐
30. Mine mål var klart definerte	☐	☐	☐	☐	☐
31. Jeg visste hvor bra jeg gjorde det ut fra hvordan jeg presterte	☐	☐	☐	☐	☐
32. Jeg var fullstendig fokusert på oppgaven jeg hadde foran meg	☐	☐	☐	☐	☐
33. Jeg følte jeg hadde full kontroll over meg selv	☐	☐	☐	☐	☐
34. Jeg bekymret meg ikke over hva andre måtte tenke om meg	☐	☐	☐	☐	☐
35. Iblant virket det nesten som om ting skjedde i sakte film	☐	☐	☐	☐	☐
36. Jeg fant opplevelsen ekstremt givende	☐	☐	☐	☐	☐

	Svært sjeldent 1	Sjeldent 2	Noen ganger 3	Ofte 4	Svært ofte 5
37. Hvor ofte opplever du at jobben din er så engasjerende?	☐	☐	☐	☐	☐

Før du fortsetter: Kontroller at du har svart på alle spørsmålene på denne sida!

Husk: Bare ett kryss på hvert spørsmål!

OPPLEVELSE AV MOTIVASJON I JOBBEN

3. Ta stilling til disse påstandene:

	Svært uenig 1	Uenig 2	Verken /eller 3	Enig 4	Svært enig 5
1. Når jeg gjør jobben min bra gir det meg en følelse av å ha prestert noe	☐	☐	☐	☐	☐
2. Når jeg utfører jobben min bra, bidrar det til min personlige vekst og utvikling	☐	☐	☐	☐	☐
3. Når jeg gjør jobben min bra gir det meg en sterk følelse av personlig tilfredshet	☐	☐	☐	☐	☐
4. Å gjøre jobben min bra gir meg bedre selvtillit	☐	☐	☐	☐	☐

OPPLEVELSE AV TILFREDSHET I JOBBEN

4. Ta stilling til disse påstandene:

	Svært uenig 1	Uenig 2	Verken /eller 3	Enig 4	Svært enig 5
1. Generelt sett er jeg svært fornøyd med denne jobben	☐	☐	☐	☐	☐
2. Jeg tenker ofte på å slutte i denne jobben	☐	☐	☐	☐	☐
3. Jeg er generelt sett fornøyd med den type arbeid jeg gjør i denne jobben	☐	☐	☐	☐	☐

OM JOBBEN DIN

5. Nevn kort de fem viktigste arbeidsoppgavene du har i jobben din.
Bruk STORE, TYDELIGE BLOKKBOKSTAVER, og bare ett tegn i hvert felt.

Oppgave 1:
Oppgave 2:
Oppgave 3:
Oppgave 4:
Oppgave 5:

	Svært dårlig 1	Dårlig 2	Både /og 3	Godt 4	Svært godt 5
6. Når du tar disse fem arbeidsoppgavene i betraktning, hvor godt synes du generelt at du utfører jobben din?	☐	☐	☐	☐	☐

7. Tenk på en typisk arbeidsdag. I hvilken grad stemmer disse påstandene for deg?

	Svært uenig 1	Uenig 2	Verken /eller 3	Enig 4	Svært enig 5
1. Jeg setter meg alltid klare mål for hvordan arbeidsoppgavene skal utføres	☐	☐	☐	☐	☐
2. Jeg har helt klare mål på hva det endelige resultatet av mine arbeidsoppgaver skal være	☐	☐	☐	☐	☐
3. Jeg har alltid klare mål på hva som skal gjøres, men jeg må ofte justere disse målene	☐	☐	☐	☐	☐
4. Denne bedriften har klare og eksakte målsettinger for sin virksomhet	☐	☐	☐	☐	☐

Før du fortsetter: Kontroller at du har svart på alle spørsmålene på denne sida!

Husk: Bare ett kryss på hvert spørsmål!

	Svært uenig 1	Uenig 2	Verken /eller 3	Enig 4	Svært enig 5

5. Jeg kommer ofte på jobb uten å ha klare mål for hva jeg skal gjøre i løpet av dagen .... ☐ ☐ ☐ ☐ ☐
6. Jeg føler meg trygg på at mine personlige mål i jobben stemmer overens med bedriftens overordnede mål .... ☐ ☐ ☐ ☐ ☐
7. Alle som jobber her er kjent med bedriftens overordnede mål .... ☐ ☐ ☐ ☐ ☐
8. Mine personlige mål på hvordan jeg skal gjøre jobben min står ofte i konflikt til bedriftens overordnede mål .... ☐ ☐ ☐ ☐ ☐
9. Målene for hvordan vi skal jobbe i denne bedriften er klart definerte .... ☐ ☐ ☐ ☐ ☐

	Aldri 1	Sjeldent 2	Noen ganger 3	Ofte 4	Svært ofte 5

10. Hvor ofte er ditt arbeid styrt av klare målsettinger på en vanlig arbeidsdag? .... ☐ ☐ ☐ ☐ ☐

DINE VURDERINGER AV DEG SELV

8. Nedenfor finner du en del påstander som passer mer eller mindre godt for ulike mennesker. Hvor godt stemmer disse påstandene for deg, slik du vanligvis er?

	Svært uenig 1	Uenig 2	Verken /eller 3	Enig 4	Svært enig 5

1. Jeg nyter å hanskes med problemer som er helt nye for meg .... ☐ ☐ ☐ ☐ ☐
2. Jeg nyter å forsøke å løse kompliserte problemer .... ☐ ☐ ☐ ☐ ☐
3. Jo vanskeligere problem, dess mer nyter jeg å forsøke å løse det .... ☐ ☐ ☐ ☐ ☐
4. Jeg vil at mitt arbeid skal gi meg muligheter til å øke mine kunnskaper og evner .... ☐ ☐ ☐ ☐ ☐
5. Nysgjerrighet er drivkraften bak mye av det jeg gjør .... ☐ ☐ ☐ ☐ ☐
6. Når jeg deltar i en aktivitet, har jeg en tendens til å bli så involvert at jeg "glemmer tiden" .... ☐ ☐ ☐ ☐ ☐
7. Når jeg er intenst interessert i noe, skal det mye til for å avbryte meg .... ☐ ☐ ☐ ☐ ☐
8. Mine venner vil beskrive meg som "ekstremt intens" når jeg er midt oppe i noe .... ☐ ☐ ☐ ☐ ☐
9. Jeg tror på betydningen av kunst .... ☐ ☐ ☐ ☐ ☐
10. Jeg elsker å komme på nye måter å gjøre ting på .... ☐ ☐ ☐ ☐ ☐
11. Jeg liker å høre om nye ideer .... ☐ ☐ ☐ ☐ ☐
12. Jeg kan løfte en samtale til et høyere nivå .... ☐ ☐ ☐ ☐ ☐
13. Jeg foretrekker variasjon framfor rutine .... ☐ ☐ ☐ ☐ ☐
14. Jeg liker å løse kompliserte problemer .... ☐ ☐ ☐ ☐ ☐
15. Jeg mestrer de fleste oppgaver .... ☐ ☐ ☐ ☐ ☐
16. Jeg kan utføre en rekke ulike oppgaver .... ☐ ☐ ☐ ☐ ☐
17. Jeg møter gjerne utfordrende oppgaver .... ☐ ☐ ☐ ☐ ☐
18. Jeg vet hvordan jeg skal anvende mine kunnskaper .... ☐ ☐ ☐ ☐ ☐

På de neste sidene blir du bedt om å tenke på noen konkrete situasjoner som kan forekomme i din jobb, og å beskrive hvordan du opplevde dette.

Før du fortsetter: Kontroller at du har svart på alle spørsmålene på denne sida!

Husk: Bare ett kryss på hvert spørsmål!

9. Tenk igjen på en konkret situasjon i jobben da du ble engasjert og helt "oppslukt" av den oppgaven du gjorde. Beskriv kort hvilken arbeidsoppgave du tenker på:
   (*Bruk* STORE, TYDELIGE BLOKKBOKSTAVER, *og bare ett tegn i hvert felt*)

10. Hvordan opplevde du denne situasjonen? *Sett ett kryss mellom hvert ordpar.*

		1	2	3	4	5	6	7	
1.	Uinteressant	☐	☐	☐	☐	☐	☐	☐	Interessant
2.	Ubehagelig	☐	☐	☐	☐	☐	☐	☐	Behagelig
3.	Vanskelig	☐	☐	☐	☐	☐	☐	☐	Lett/Enkel
4.	Utfordrende	☐	☐	☐	☐	☐	☐	☐	Tam
5.	Trist	☐	☐	☐	☐	☐	☐	☐	Fylt av glede
6.	Dramatisk	☐	☐	☐	☐	☐	☐	☐	Udramatisk
7.	Kjedelig	☐	☐	☐	☐	☐	☐	☐	Morsom

11. Hvor godt synes du at du klarte å utføre arbeidsoppgaven du beskrev ovenfor?

Svært dårlig 1	Dårlig 2	Både /og 3	Godt 4	Svært godt 5
☐	☐	☐	☐	☐

12. Hvor ofte opplever du en slik situasjon i din jobb?

Svært sjeldent 1	Sjeldent 2	Noen ganger 3	Ofte 4	Svært ofte 5
☐	☐	☐	☐	☐

13. Hvor motivert følte du deg da du utførte arbeidsoppgaven du beskrev ovenfor?

Svært u-motivert 1	U-motivert 2	Verken /eller 3	Motivert 4	Svært motivert 5
☐	☐	☐	☐	☐

14. Hvor fornøyd følte du deg med arbeidet ditt etter at du hadde jobbet med denne oppgaven?

Svært mis-fornøyd 1	Mis-fornøyd 2	Verken /eller 3	Fornøyd 4	Svært fornøyd 5
☐	☐	☐	☐	☐

Før du fortsetter: Kontroller at du har svart på alle spørsmålene på denne sida!

Husk: Bare ett kryss på hvert spørsmål!

15. Tenk på en konkret situasjon i jobben hvor du følte deg veldig presset på tiden og var nødt til å få ferdig en arbeidsoppgave. Beskriv kort hvilken arbeidsoppgave du tenker på:
(*Bruk* STORE, TYDELIGE BLOKKBOKSTAVER, *og bare ett tegn i hvert felt*)

16. Hvordan opplevde du denne situasjonen?

		1	2	3	4	5	6	7	
1.	Uinteressant	☐	☐	☐	☐	☐	☐	☐	Interessant
2.	Ubehagelig	☐	☐	☐	☐	☐	☐	☐	Behagelig
3.	Vanskelig	☐	☐	☐	☐	☐	☐	☐	Lett/Enkel
4.	Utfordrende	☐	☐	☐	☐	☐	☐	☐	Tam
5.	Trist	☐	☐	☐	☐	☐	☐	☐	Fylt av glede
6.	Dramatisk	☐	☐	☐	☐	☐	☐	☐	Udramatisk
7.	Kjedelig	☐	☐	☐	☐	☐	☐	☐	Morsom

17. Hvor godt synes du at du klarte å utføre arbeidsoppgaven du beskrev ovenfor?

Svært dårlig 1	Dårlig 2	Både /og 3	Godt 4	Svært godt 5
☐	☐	☐	☐	☐

18. Hvor ofte opplever du en slik situasjon i din jobb?

Svært sjeldent 1	Sjeldent 2	Noen ganger 3	Ofte 4	Svært ofte 5
☐	☐	☐	☐	☐

19. Hvor motivert følte du deg da du utførte arbeidsoppgaven du beskrev ovenfor?

Svært u-motivert 1	U-motivert 2	Verken /eller 3	Motivert 4	Svært motivert 5
☐	☐	☐	☐	☐

20. Hvor fornøyd følte du deg med arbeidet ditt etter at du hadde jobbet med denne oppgaven?

Svært mis-fornøyd 1	Mis-fornøyd 2	Verken /eller 3	Fornøyd 4	Svært fornøyd 5
☐	☐	☐	☐	☐

Før du fortsetter: Kontroller at du har svart på alle spørsmålene på denne sida!

Husk: Bare ett kryss på hvert spørsmål!

21. Tenk på en konkret situasjon i jobben hvor du hadde god tid til å gjøre ferdig den oppgaven du holdt på med. Beskriv kort hvilken arbeidsoppgave du tenker på:
    (*Bruk STORE, TYDELIGE BLOKKBOKSTAVER, og bare ett tegn i hvert felt*)

22. Hvordan opplevde du denne situasjonen?

		1	2	3	4	5	6	7	
1.	Uinteressant	☐	☐	☐	☐	☐	☐	☐	Interessant
2.	Ubehagelig	☐	☐	☐	☐	☐	☐	☐	Behagelig
3.	Vanskelig	☐	☐	☐	☐	☐	☐	☐	Lett/Enkel
4.	Utfordrende	☐	☐	☐	☐	☐	☐	☐	Tam
5.	Trist	☐	☐	☐	☐	☐	☐	☐	Fylt av glede
6.	Dramatisk	☐	☐	☐	☐	☐	☐	☐	Udramatisk
7.	Kjedelig	☐	☐	☐	☐	☐	☐	☐	Morsom

23. Hvor godt synes du at du klarte å utføre arbeidsoppgaven du beskrev ovenfor? .... Svært dårlig (1) ☐ ... Dårlig (2) ☐ ... Både /og (3) ☐ ... Godt (4) ☐ ... Svært godt (5) ☐

24. Hvor ofte opplever du en slik situasjon i din jobb?......... Svært sjeldent (1) ☐ ... Sjeldent (2) ☐ ... Noen ganger (3) ☐ ... Ofte (4) ☐ ... Svært ofte (5) ☐

25. Hvor motivert følte du deg da du utførte arbeidsoppgaven du beskrev ovenfor? .... Svært u-motivert (1) ☐ ... U-motivert (2) ☐ ... Verken /eller (3) ☐ ... Motivert (4) ☐ ... Svært motivert (5) ☐

26. Hvor fornøyd følte du deg med arbeidet ditt etter at du hadde jobbet med denne oppgaven? .... Svært misfornøyd (1) ☐ ... Misfornøyd (2) ☐ ... Verken /eller (3) ☐ ... Fornøyd (4) ☐ ... Svært fornøyd (5) ☐

Før du fortsetter: Kontroller at du har svart på alle spørsmålene på denne sida!

Husk: Bare ett kryss på hvert spørsmål!

27. Tenk på en konkret situasjon i jobben hvor du ikke lyktes i å nå målene du hadde satt deg til en oppgave. Beskriv kort hvilken arbeidsoppgave du tenker på:
    (Bruk STORE, TYDELIGE BLOKKBOKSTAVER, og bare ett tegn i hvert felt)

28. Hvordan opplevde du denne situasjonen?

		1	2	3	4	5	6	7	
1.	Uinteressant	☐	☐	☐	☐	☐	☐	☐	Interessant
2.	Ubehagelig	☐	☐	☐	☐	☐	☐	☐	Behagelig
3.	Vanskelig	☐	☐	☐	☐	☐	☐	☐	Lett/Enkel
4.	Utfordrende	☐	☐	☐	☐	☐	☐	☐	Tam
5.	Trist	☐	☐	☐	☐	☐	☐	☐	Fylt av glede
6.	Dramatisk	☐	☐	☐	☐	☐	☐	☐	Udramatisk
7.	Kjedelig	☐	☐	☐	☐	☐	☐	☐	Morsom

29. Hvor godt synes du at du klarte å utføre arbeidsoppgaven du beskrev ovenfor?

Svært dårlig 1	Dårlig 2	Både /og 3	Godt 4	Svært godt 5
☐	☐	☐	☐	☐

30. Hvor ofte opplever du en slik situasjon i din jobb?

Svært sjeldent 1	Sjeldent 2	Noen ganger 3	Ofte 4	Svært ofte 5
☐	☐	☐	☐	☐

31. Hvor motivert følte du deg da du utførte arbeidsoppgaven du beskrev ovenfor?

Svært u-motivert 1	U-motivert 2	Verken /eller 3	Motivert 4	Svært motivert 5
☐	☐	☐	☐	☐

32. Hvor fornøyd følte du deg med arbeidet ditt etter at du hadde jobbet med denne oppgaven?

Svært mis-fornøyd 1	Mis-fornøyd 2	Verken /eller 3	Fornøyd 4	Svært fornøyd 5
☐	☐	☐	☐	☐

Plass for kommentarer:

Takk for at du ville svare på spørsmålene!